JACK THORNE

Jack Thorne's plays for the stage include *Hope* (Royal Court Theatre, London, 2014); adaptations of *Let the Right One In* (National Theatre of Scotland at Dundee Rep, the Royal Court and the Apollo Theatre, London, 2013/14) and *Stuart: A Life Backwards* (Underbelly, Edinburgh, and tour, 2013); *Mydidae* (Soho, 2012; Trafalgar Studios, 2013); an adaptation of Friedrich Dürrenmatt's *The Physicists* (Donmar Warehouse, 2012); *Bunny* (Underbelly, Edinburgh, 2010; Soho, 2011); *2nd May 1997* (Bush, 2009); *Burying Your Brother in the Pavement* (National Theatre Connections, 2008); *When You Cure Me* (Bush, 2005; Radio 3's Drama on Three, 2006); *Fanny and Faggot* (Pleasance, Edinburgh, 2004 and 2007; Finborough, 2007; English Theatre of Bruges, 2007; Trafalgar Studios, 2007); and *Stacy* (Tron, 2006; Arcola, 2007; Trafalgar Studios, 2007). His radio plays include *Left at the Angel* (Radio 4, 2007), an adaptation of *The Hunchback of Notre Dame* (2009) and an original play *People Snogging in Public Places* (Radio 3's Wire slot, 2009). He was a core writer in all three series of *Skins* (E4, Channel 4, BBC America), writing five episodes. His other TV writing includes *Glue*, *The Fades* (2012 BAFTA for Best Drama Series), *Shameless, Cast-Offs, This is England '86* (2011 Royal Television Society Award for Best Writer – Drama), *This is England '88, This is England '90* and the thirty-minute drama *The Spastic King*. His work for film includes the features *A Long Way Down*, adapted from Nick Hornby's novel, and *The Scouting Book for Boys*, which won him the Star of London Best Newcomer Award at the London Film Festival 2009.

JACK THORNE

Plays: One

When You Cure Me
Stacy
2nd May 1997
Bunny
Red Car, Blue Car
Mydidae

with an Introduction by the author

NICK HERN BOOKS
London
www.nickhernbooks.co.uk

A Nick Hern Book

Jack Thorne Plays: One first published in Great Britain as a paperback original in 2014 by Nick Hern Books Limited, The Glasshouse, 49a Goldhawk Road, London W12 8QP

This collection copyright © 2014 Jack Thorne
Introduction copyright © 2014 Jack Thorne

When You Cure Me copyright © 2005, 2014 Jack Thorne
Stacy copyright © 2007, 2014 Jack Thorne
2nd May 1997 copyright © 2009, 2014 Jack Thorne
Bunny © 2010, 2014 Jack Thorne
Red Car, Blue Car copyright © 2014 Jack Thorne
Mydidae copyright © 2012, 2014 Jack Thorne

Bunny illustrations copyright © 2010 Jenny Turner (www.jenny-turner.co.uk)

Jack Thorne has asserted his right to be identified as the author of these works

Cover image © Jenny Turner

Designed and typeset by Nick Hern Books, London
Printed in Great Britain by CPI Group (UK) Ltd

ISBN 978 1 84842 448 7

For Rachel Mason,
who changed everything

Contents

Introduction

So this is probably the most intimidating thing I've ever written.

I think I started writing plays as a way of expressing the things that I couldn't say. I'm a constant idiot in conversation – I always seem to sound either smug or stupid. Writing plays was a way of winning the conversation by controlling the conversation. I became 'super talk' – the king of all arguments – impressing everyone with my wit and vivacity. Sadly, none of those plays were any good. I then went through a stage of utter self-hatred and destruction – where everything I wrote was about how disgusting I was as a human being and how much I hated the world and particularly me within the world. Those plays were still largely shit, but were slightly better. And then I think – I hope – I learnt how to write about other people – and then I think – I hope – I learnt how to write about myself again with a better sense of balance. Because these plays are, apologies in advance, overwhelmingly about me.

Anyway, this is my *Plays: One* but I'd written about twenty-two plays before the first play in this volume. I occasionally get them out and have a read – thinking maybe there's a thought or an idea or even a turn of phrase that I could use for something new. There's not. They're dire. Even now I'm not quite sure why I persevered. Everyone told me to do something else – the criticism was wide-ranging, but mostly very critical. My endurance was partly due to love and partly due to utter dependence. I wrote my first play because I wanted to direct something at university and couldn't afford the £65-a-night amateur fees. And from the moment I started writing, it was instant, I grew slightly obsessive about it. I was a terrible writer, but utterly obsessive. Before I got married I was a sixteen-hour-a-day, seven-days-a-week man. Now I'm ten-hours-a-day and my wife and I have a contract which states that I take at least half a day off a week. All of which is to say, I am entirely psychologically dependent on writing, it gives me stability when all else is failing. And I spend way too much time doing it.

I was taught, as many others were, by Simon Stephens as part of the Royal Court Young Writers' Programme. He taught us all a huge amount, but there was one thing he said in particular which I've puzzled over ever since – that every writer has a myth. A story that they return to again and again – something which drives them – something which gives their plays a sense of themselves. That it's not a writer's job to identify his or her myth but that it's there – in the background – if you look for it. Simon, when I asked him, said, after quite a lot of thinking, he thought his own myth was probably 'listen to children' – though he said he wasn't sure and other people might be better judges, and when I've mentioned it to him since he had no recollection of thinking that. But watching his work through the prism of 'listen to children' I've found quite a beautiful experience. I don't know what my myth is, and I'd struggle to nail it down, but I think it has something to do with help – what help is, and the struggle we all go through trying to help others, and perhaps what failure to help looks and feels like. Like I say, I could be wrong. And it feels self-important even guessing at it. But there is something about thinking that there's something I'm trying to say – that I have a myth – that's always felt somehow useful to me. Both in looking at others and worrying about myself.

The first time I thought I might have a future as a writer was as a result of a phone call from an amazing woman called Teresa Topolski (who *Bunny* is dedicated to). I'd been sending off letters to theatres for a while, and unsurprisingly not getting very encouraging letters back. In fact, I once got the opportunity to look through the Bush Theatre's 'reader pile' and discovered the notes written on my first play I sent them which concluded with 'This play is, on the whole, irritating.' But Tessa thankfully saw something even in these terrible irritating plays – and called me up – this is the days before mobile phones – on my mum and dad's phone – and said she thought my plays were interesting (I'd sent the same three to her at the Tricycle) – I remember playing the message to my little sister approximately twenty-four times. Every play I subsequently wrote I sent to her, for about three years, and she constantly stayed interested and un-irritated by me. She built my confidence, she encouraged me to look at my writing in a new way. She gave me the courage to approach agents and theatres again and I managed to secure an agent who also saw something passably interesting in me – Rachel Taylor – who also proved brilliant at reading and who remains to this day the most ferocious of readers of my first drafts. And at the same time – through the Royal Court Young Writers' Programme – I fell in with another writer – Laura Wade – who became a close friend. And we set up a system where I read everything Laura wrote (and everything she wrote was, of course, brilliant) and she read everything I wrote. These three worked me hard. They were perfect readers – tearing apart that which was important to tear apart. And eventually I sent out something – then called *A Bedroom* – which they thought might actually work onstage. Tessa thought me better suited to the Bush than the Tricycle. She took it to them. And the Bush commissioned me to rewrite it, which I did under a new title, *When You Cure Me*.

When You Cure Me was written partly as a result of this illness I was struggling with. I had (actually still have) a condition called Cholinergic Urticaria. Which is a strange version of a sort of chronic prickly heat. I'm allergic to heat in all its forms – natural, artificial and body – any stimulation left me covered in painful red welts. At my worst I was lying flat in my parents' house with all the windows open – in December – in Wales – and every time I moved I was getting an allergic reaction – I was allergic to moving. It's an unknowable condition that various doctors tried me on various medications for, and it came on very suddenly when I was twenty-one and caused me to drop out of my final year of university. Which was annoying and frustrating and made me feel like a failure. Now it's under control, then it was brutal. And no one really knew how to help me with it. Friends who kindly wrote me postcards would get nine-page letters in reply, they'd write back again a week later and immediately get another nine pages, eventually I scared them all away through sheer exhaustion. My mum made me a cake a week but found my bedroom really upsetting. I was told by one doctor it was possible I might not get better, and by another that it was all in my head. I felt very very sorry for myself and angry with the world. So in the play Rachel is me, but so is Peter. And hopefully neither is me too. I think it's a play less about someone getting better, and more about someone learning how to recover, and how to help the people around her recover too.

That play was directed by Mike Bradwell, who said there were three answers to every question I can be asked as a playwright: 'yes', 'no' and 'moo'. 'Moo' was the get-out clause, the answer to the unanswerable question, or the question best left for the process rather than for the playwright's head. It's a system I still try to use to this day. I struggle quite a lot in rehearsals, partly because I'm shy, partly because I still don't really understand the work that actors and directors do. I love the magic at the end, but the getting there – the wrong turns that are necessary to make something work – I find slightly beguiling and worrying. So *When You Cure Me* remains the only play I attended every day of rehearsals for. I remember watching the dress rehearsal from the back of the room, which was too hot for me to deal with. But that press night – I've never had a feeling like it – the actors did something extraordinary and I was floored by the whole thing.

Stacy is probably the play I most struggle to talk about but it is strangely personal to me. I think it's probably about loneliness more than anything else. It was written concurrently with *When You Cure Me* but over a much longer period of time. I was living in Croydon with my brother while I was writing it, still ill, still unsure how to be, and I had decided I didn't really need friends. I mean, *any* friends. It was an odd decision that made me slightly odd. Not that I'm capable of those acts that Rob does in the play, but that feeling of utter hopelessness and hatred to all others, I think is one I recognise from that time. Writing it, I think I was thinking a lot about Cambridge University, which I went to and didn't have a very good time at. I went from a comprehensive school where I was known as being a kid who academically excelled, and found myself in a very exclusive environment full of very exclusively educated people, most of whom made me feel like a failure. For me, that's the tragedy of Oxbridge – everyone that goes there goes defined by their cleverness and – surrounded by the cleverness of others – they feel their identity taken from them – and they drown. Or maybe that was just my experience. I think *Stacy* is about a drowning man who does something horrific. Something unforgiveable. I hope it never attempts to justify him and I really hope it doesn't pity him. Bizarrely, it's my mum's favourite play. Read it with that in your head: 'His mother really likes this one.' It'll make it an even more disgusting read.

Hamish Pirie and I actually had the opportunity to make the show twice – with two different actors. Arthur Darvill and then Ralf Little. It's the biggest lesson I've ever learnt about what actors bring to roles. Because the two of them couldn't have been further apart. Arthur was this beautiful mess of odd angles, wonderfully eccentric and deeply upsetting; Ralf, in contrast, looked the audience dead in the eye and pulled his skin off. Both did something magical. It was a quite extraordinary time.

I have tried, and am currently engaged in, trying to write an explicitly political play which expresses how I feel about politics. I find doing so very very embarrassing and exposing, mostly because it involves, as you can see from the previous sentence, a lot of the word 'I'. I'm very nervous, as I think a lot of writers are, by the notion of the play as a soapbox. Those are the sort of shows I want to walk out of (I've never had the confidence to walk out of any of them, mind you).

2nd May 1997 was and is my attempt to write a political play without the politics. I was very involved in the Labour Party at the time, and, whilst delivering leaflets for the European elections, two different people came out of their houses to give them back. Saying we were all as bad as each other and they wouldn't be voting. I found this very difficult. I grew up in a political household and engaging in politics was always seen as important. But more than that, I grew up admiring political people, of all colours. I like people who want to be heard. I'd also been reflecting quite a lot on Tony Blair and what he meant, because no one had broken my heart quite as he had. I have to this day his first election poster on his wall. Why? Because those May 1997 elections were quite an extraordinary thing to be part of, not that I'd done much. I'd delivered some leaflets for Martin Salter in Reading West (an election he won) and I'd stood for my school elections for the Labour Party (an election which I'd lost). I wanted to tell the story of that election from all sides. I was also frustrated by my inability to write a play about anyone else but me, so doing a triptych – inspired by David Eldridge's *Under the Blue Sky* – felt like an opportunity to force myself outside of my comfort zone. Three political parties, three love stories, one night.

The starting point for writing it was a play I'd written for nabokov's new-writing night, 'Present: Tense'. A two-hander about choice, which George Perrin and I worked up together. That, with a major rewrite, became the middle act, the Liberal Democrat one. The Labour one I always knew would be less of a struggle, I could safely write myself into that one. The Conservative story, which would become the first act, was the one that I lost sleep over. Although I'm a passionate Labour Party supporter, I didn't want it to be a cheap point-scoring battle, I wanted it to be rather a way of telling the story of the tragedy of those men and women (mostly men) whose life had been defined by the Conservative Party and who were watching a landslide wipe away what they'd understood of their life, a rejection which must have felt so foreign to them after eighteen solid years of power. I still don't think I've got it right, but I must have rewritten that act, with different characters, twenty or thirty times.

I'd sort of disappeared into TV and film when the opportunity for *Bunny* came around. It was quite easy for me to be seduced by screen, I find writing screenplays a lot easier than writing for the stage, I find the joy of being able to describe camera movement, of being able to write 'cut to', just wonderful things – and these are tools stage writers don't have. Maybe it's because I largely grew up watching TV rather than going to theatre, but for me – to this day – there is nothing harder than the blank page of the first draft of a stage play. So when Joe Murphy came to me with the idea of writing a play for nabokov, I initially baulked at the idea. Scared of going back to it all.

Bunny is my love note to Luton. Once I left my brother's place in Croydon, I lived in Luton for seven-and-a-half years until my wife told me, quite flatly, she wasn't going to move there. And people may not immediately see it, but the truth is, Luton is a wonderful town. I certainly would never have left, had my wife not made me. Maybe it's that element of 'Everyone hates us, but we don't care.' Maybe living there is the equivalent of supporting Millwall. But it's always been – and seems like it will always be – a town with a lot of complication within it. My local Post Office was run by a Pakistani gentleman, and twice I was standing in the queue behind two different young kids, looking quite confused about life, wearing English Defence League tops. The strange thing is, both were polite to the Pakistani shopkeeper, and he was polite back. I wanted to tell a story about that racial complication. How it's not about race per se, but something much more intricate than that. We've kept Jenny Turner's illustrations in the book, because the illustrations made so much difference to how we told the story. They're wonderful.

Red Car, Blue Car came out of my time at the Bush, the only place that's ever felt like a theatrical home to me. If such a thing is possible. When the time came to move from the old building to the new, the great Josie Rourke wanted to work out what the theatre could do, so she commissioned three writers to write three plays which could be staged in three different ways. To make things more complicated, she also gave us a set of props we had to include, and had luminaries of the theatre nominate stage directions which we had to include in the text. I cheated slightly by absorbing these into spoken word, but Tom Wells, one of the other writers, went all out, and his play was this truly magical maniacal thing.

There's a strange thing when you're set limits. It was in an Alan Ayckbourn collection that I read that the reason why Norman doesn't appear in the first act of the first play of *The Norman Conquests* is because the actor he wanted to play Norman wasn't available for the first week of rehearsals. Isn't that brilliant? In my opinion, one of the finest contemporary comedies of my age – and someone not being around for a week of rehearsals changed the entire way it felt. I'm not saying that limits are always a good thing, mostly they're terrible, but sometimes limits can be the making of you. I wasn't sure whether to include *Red Car, Blue Car* in this volume, but I actually think it might be one of the better-written plays.

The final play in the collection is *Mydidae*. Which came out of my obsession with Phoebe Waller-Bridge. I love actors. In fact, I get weird obsessions with certain actors – Morven Christie, Mat Fraser, Johnny Harris, and Phoebe amongst many others. They're part of a certain breed of actors – actors that feel a little dangerous – that feel like they could do anything. Phoebe can do amazing things with a line, but what's astonishing about her, for me, is how incredibly cruel she can seem and how exposed she's capable of making herself when perpetuating that cruelty. She's also very funny. She and Vicky Jones came to me with a commission to write a play set in a bathroom. I thought I might enjoy that and said yes as long as Phoebe would be in it. I told Phoebe that a bathroom, her choice, might involve more than a little exposure on the actor's part – and she said something like: 'Yes, darling, understood, everything's on the table, though try to avoid the labia if you could.' Vicky and her are best friends and a formidable double act. They sort of think with the same head, albeit one that can argue with itself. I learnt a lot about their version of femininity through the process, and found myself challenged in lots of ways I wasn't expecting to be.

I think it's less a play about intimacy than about fear of intimacy. It's a play about exposing your wounds to someone else and hoping they don't say 'You're horrendous.' It's a play that I wrote and then rewrote and rewrote. The last draft I started in Sweden attending a wedding, with my girlfriend in tow, and a month after finishing it, just as we were starting to rehearse, I asked my girlfriend to marry me. She's now my wife, Rachel, and the woman to whom this collection is dedicated, even though most of it was written before we were together. She now knows more about me than anyone ever has, and I probably know more about her and she doesn't hate me for that knowledge of my insides, despite my presumption she would, and we're still doing okay. So more than anything, probably as bizarre as it seems when you read it, *Mydidae* is a play about falling in love or, perhaps more than that, working out you are in love. And that being in love is scary but okay.

So, to sum up – largely these plays – as a whole – are about the journey of a lonely ill man to a man who's still a little ill but very much not alone. They could also be about someone getting happy. I hope that doesn't sound self-indulgent. I would like – and am trying – to write plays that are less about me in the future – but these plays – my first good ones – are mostly about where I am – or was – at. For better or worse. I hope you enjoy them. I've loved writing them.

Jack Thorne
September 2014

WHEN YOU CURE ME

For Chris Thorne and Fiona Bleach

When You Cure Me was first performed at the Bush Theatre, London, on 16 November 2005, with the following cast:

PETER	Samuel Barnett
RACHEL	Morven Christie
JAMES	Daniel Bayle
ALICE	Lisa McDonald
ANGELA	Gwyneth Strong

Director	Mike Bradwell
Designer	Penelope Challen
Lighting Designer	Tanya Burns
Sound Designer	Nick Manning

When You Cure Me received its first workshops as part of the National Youth Theatre's Short Nyts season in August 2004, directed by Vicky Jones. The play was subsequently commissioned by the Bush Theatre.

4

Characters

PETER, *seventeen*
RACHEL, *seventeen*
JAMES, *seventeen*
ALICE, *seventeen*
ANGELA, *forty-two*

Set

A teenage girl's bedroom. The play takes place in Reading over a period of three months, from January to March.

Rachel's Injuries

Rachel has a long inflamed scar down the side of her face. Surrounding the scar is severe bruising that puffs her eye. The cut gets less inflamed as the play progresses and by Act Four there's no bruising at all, just the scar. Stiffness in the rest of her body also gradually dissipates. In particular, in Act One she has trouble with her left hand and wrist but by Act Three she's moving it as if normal. But the main damage sustained is that Rachel can't move her legs, and has very little movement in the base to the middle of her spine. She is bedbound and moving her body is very painful because the rest of her spine is forced to take a weight and pressure it's not used to, but she does have some movement and some control of her bowels.

ACT ONE

1.1

17th January.

In the blackout.

PETER (*soft, so soft*). You awake...

The lights rise gently. She's not awake, she's just sort of stretching her mouth, so he sits back. This takes for ever.

She moves again.

Rach...

Pause.

Rach...

Pause.

(*Louder.*) Rachel...

Pause. The lights are at full brightness.

Rachel, you awake...

RACHEL. Wha...

PETER (*reaching out and touching her arm again, his hand rests on the side of the bed*). Hi.

Pause.

Rachel?

RACHEL. Uh... Di' you?

She retches like she's about to throw up, but stops herself.

Pause.

PETER. Bad dream, or...

RACHEL (*takes his hand in hers*). No.

Pause. He tries to take his hand away, but he doesn't know how.

I need to pee…

PETER. Okay.

RACHEL. I, uh…

PETER. Shall I call your mum or…

RACHEL. No. Don't call her.

PETER. Okay. Are you…

RACHEL. Can you do it?

PETER. Really? Sure.

RACHEL. There's a pan under the bed.

PETER. Okay.

He grasps under the bed, which is pretty cluttered, for the bedpan.

(*Desperately casual.*) What does it look like?

RACHEL. Blue.

PETER. Yeah.

He re-emerges with it.

RACHEL. There should be a, there's a insert under there too – just cardboard – there's a stack of them – they just slot in – the insert should…

He finds the cardboard insert.

PETER. Is this…

RACHEL. Yeah. Pass it here, it sort of clips in.

PETER. No. I can do it…

He inserts it clumsily and then he goes to the end of the bed and lifts her legs, quite roughly. He's improvising and being slightly rough with it, so that when he attempts to slide the bedpan underneath, she immediately falls off.

RACHEL (*warning*). Peter…

PETER. Am I… What?

RACHEL. You're being rough… a bit…

PETER. Oh…

Beat.

RACHEL. Um. My knickers…

PETER. Yeah.

He does so gently, and blindly, sliding them off her by the knicker-straps, and being careful not to look. Then he holds the knickers, unsure of what to do with them.

RACHEL. Do you want to… get Mum…

PETER (*puts the knickers in his pocket with confidence*). It's okay.

He hesitates and then gently lifts her legs and slides the bedpan on.

RACHEL. You have to keep hold of me, so I don't – Sorry, I don't want to slip off.

PETER. No. No. It's fine.

RACHEL. I just don't want Mum sniffing…

PETER. It's fine. I'm pleased.

He holds her by the hips, trying to keep this as non-sexual as possible. From the floor below we faintly hear the sound of The Archers *theme music kicking off.*

Pause. She hasn't started peeing yet, she's sweating slightly, this is very difficult.

Okay?

RACHEL. Yeah.

Pause.

I'm slipping, grip tighter…

PETER. Like this.

RACHEL. Yeah.

PETER *tightens and doesn't know which way to look, so he just looks at her, and she stares at him and they're stuck like this and it's perfect and horrible. Then, finally, she starts to pee. It's hard for her to pee, and she only gives up a pathetic amount, but it seems to make a huge clattering noise as it dribbles into the cardboard bedpan.* PETER *doesn't breathe until she finishes.*

You need to get me the toilet tissue.

PETER. Is that...? Are you balanced?

RACHEL (*moves her own hands in order to steady herself*). Yeah.

He gently lets go, leaving her balancing on the bedpan whilst he finds the toilet paper. He finds it.

PETER. Do you...

RACHEL. Yeah. Give it here.

He hands her the toilet roll, she wipes herself whilst looking precariously balanced. He moves as if to help at one point, but holds back. She deposits the tissue in the bedpan.

You empty it in the toilet – and there's a bin in there – for the, uh, insert.

PETER. Okay...

He reaches in again, helps her balance herself, and then slides her off the bedpan.

RACHEL. Don't look at it – there'll be blood...

PETER. Okay.

He takes the bedpan out of the room, carefully averting his eyes. We're left with just her. She shifts on the bed and winces. She touches the scar on her cheek, she traces it with her fingers. She tries to shift up on the bed, but she winces again and gags, this really hurts.

(*Re-entering.*) Okay...

RACHEL. Yeah.

PETER sits by her bed. They sit in silence, then she takes his hand.

PETER. There wasn't much blood.

RACHEL. Wasn't there?

PETER. I thought you'd want to know – there wasn't…

Beat. She watches him.

RACHEL. You need to give me my knickers back…

PETER (*laughs through his nose*). Yeah. Um…

He finds the knickers in his pocket and starts putting them on her legs. He's rough again, like he was with the first attempt at the bedpan. She waits until he finishes and then moves her own hands down to straighten up his attempts.

They sit in silence for a moment.

I could get you some of those Baby Wipes. For your hands, so that when you go to the loo, you can clean them too. Because you don't want them dirty – I thought –

RACHEL. Okay.

PETER. I'll get them tonight. When I leave… or…

RACHEL. Yeah. Okay.

PETER. Just say when you've had enough basically…

Pause.

RACHEL. I'm really pleased… you're here.

PETER. Yeah? I spoke to James last night…

RACHEL. Okay.

PETER. He asked after you. He sounded worried.

RACHEL (*non-committal*). Okay.

PETER. They've got back together, him and Alice. He sounded really pleased about it, she said some really nice stuff to him too, about it all…

RACHEL. Okay.

They sit in silence again. PETER *takes a Ventolin asthma inhaler from his trousers and takes a squirt.*

PETER. Everyone's being really nice about it… you. I mean, everyone's saying nice things…

RACHEL (*soft*). There's no reason, for the legs – it's just me –

PETER. Yeah?

RACHEL. It'll go away –

PETER. Okay.

RACHEL. They think it'll go away soon – sometimes it just does – they basically promised. Will you help me sit up…

PETER. Yeah. You just want another cushion behind you or…

RACHEL. No. Just sitting up…

PETER. Okay.

He leans over her, and holds her by her armpits. He starts to haul her up the bed, so she's higher on the headboard. But then she screams and he stops. He doesn't speak, he just makes a noise.

Pause.

RACHEL (*getting her breath back*). It's fine.

Pause.

PETER. I didn't –

RACHEL. It's fine.

Pause. They both get their breath back.

Pull me up a bit higher, would you?

PETER. What? No! It hurts you.

RACHEL. I want to be up higher.

PETER. No, I…

RACHEL. Please, Peter.

PETER. Why?

RACHEL. Can you help me, please?

He gingerly fingers his arms around her armpits and attempts to pull her higher on the headboard. He starts carefully, but he has to tug her up, so he can't be gentle. She gags slightly at the effort, but manages to stop herself from screaming.

(*Again waiting a moment for breath.*) Thank you.

They sit a moment longer. PETER is white-faced. He pulls out and takes another tug from his inhaler.

PETER. Are you okay?

RACHEL. I feel older, do you know that?

PETER. Yeah? I don't particularly. Is that –

Beat.

RACHEL. Will you get in with me?

PETER. Yeah?

RACHEL. Will you...

PETER. It won't hurt?

RACHEL. No.

Beat.

PETER. That wasn't what that was about, was it? Getting up higher.

RACHEL. No.

PETER. You weren't making it so I could get in. Moving up, so...

RACHEL. Will you get in?

PETER. Yeah.

He squeezes himself onto the bed, so that his hips are just on the side of the bed. She pulls him in closer, and partly curls what parts of the body she can around him.

Can you, uh –

RACHEL. This is nice.

PETER. Yeah.

RACHEL. I can feel your heartbeat, it's going quick actually…

PETER. Is it?

RACHEL. Yeah. (*Takes his hand and puts it on his heart.*)

PETER. Yeah.

RACHEL. You're nervous, that's all –

Beat.

(*Soft.*) Do you mind the scar?

PETER. No.

RACHEL. It'll fade. I mean, I'll look the same…

PETER. You're really pretty. You still are.

Beat.

RACHEL. This is nice. I like it like this.

She feels her hand around and sort of pats him.

PETER (*giggle*). Oh. Um. Mr Norris asked if you wanted work set, by the way.

She giggles.

And Mr Edwards, though he was weird about it, he said I had to talk to him, well, if I wanted to, and that I had to call him Geoff…

RACHEL (*giggle*). Geoff!

PETER (*giggle*). Yeah.

Pause. She tries to snuggle up.

RACHEL. I'm really happy just like this…

PETER. Yeah.

RACHEL. Geoff!

PETER (*giggle*). Yeah.

RACHEL. What did you do?

PETER. I don't know. Ran away.

She smiles. Pause, a long luxury pause. They breathe into each other.

RACHEL. I wish we could just stay like this…

PETER. Yeah.

Pause.

RACHEL (*suddenly whitens*). Peter. Is that… Peter. Have you got an erection?

PETER. No.

He shifts his groin backwards.

RACHEL. Yes. Ow.

PETER. No.

RACHEL. Peter – you can't – ow –

PETER. I can't – I'm sorry –

He moves his arms back, he tries to find space, he can't. She growls like a cat, pure frustration. He's almost in tears.

Sorry – I can't…

RACHEL. I can *feel* it – uh – uh –

He's trying to pull everything away from her.

PETER. Don't, don't, I'm sorry. I'm sorry.

Beat.

I'm sorry.

Beat. He's as far back as he can be, yet he still flurries some more, trying to find more space.

I'm so sorry. Rachel… Rachel…

RACHEL (*half-spoken*). Okay.

Beat. She's struggling to control her tears. He concentrates on holding his stomach in.

PETER. Sorry –

RACHEL. No.

PETER. Sorry, shall I get off –

Beat.

RACHEL. Hold me.

PETER. Sorry. I'm so sorry.

Pause. She moves towards him. He tries to evade as much of her as possible, but she's more aggressive than he is.

Pause.

RACHEL. No. Get off.

PETER. Sorry. I'm really...

He half-falls off the bed in relief.

It's not. It doesn't mean I expect... it's not like a signal or...

Beat. She can't speak. He tries to stand in a way that minimises the erection. He takes another squirt from his inhaler, he's in a panic.

I'm really really sorry, I just don't know what to do... That's all. Sorry.

Beat.

RACHEL (*swallow*). Okay.

PETER. I feel sick. I'm really sorry.

Pause. PETER can't decide whether to leave or not. He's determined not to look at the door until he does.

(*Soft, his mouth doesn't work properly.*) I'm not sure what I'm supposed to do...

Pause. He straightens his back, the erection has finally subsided.

Rachel...

Pause.

Rach…

RACHEL (*looks up finally, meets his face*). Yeah?

PETER. Sorry? Sorry.

Blackout.

1.2

21st January.

JAMES *and* ALICE *are beautiful people.* RACHEL *is enjoying them, despite herself.* PETER *is a little cluttered. All except* RACHEL *wear school uniform.*

JAMES…. He was having a go and he put his hand down her trousers and he couldn't find what he was looking for so he kept looking and then he put his finger in, but it wasn't the right hole –

RACHEL. What?

JAMES. Went for the pink and potted the brown, Mary Gill, though this isn't from either of them. Anyway, so she slapped him.

ALICE. Did she?

JAMES. Didn't I tell you this? Yeah. Apparently she slapped him.

RACHEL. Mary?

JAMES. Yeah.

ALICE. She's fancied him for ages.

JAMES (*opens his bag and brings out cheap vodka*). Well, he's not going near her now – probably not until he smelt his finger that he realised. (*Takes a swig of the vodka.*) Actually, he smelt his finger and he's either realised, or he thinks she's seriously unwell, can you drink?

RACHEL. Yeah.

PETER. What?

JAMES (*mimicking* PETER *as he hands her the bottle*). 'What?' Have you got any music?

PETER. James –

RACHEL (*to* PETER). What? (*To* JAMES.) Nothing good.

JAMES (*laughs*). I'll find something.

RACHEL. Okay.

> PETER *sits down on the side of the bed. He turns on the bedside light beside* RACHEL, *then looks around at the rest of the room and turns the light off again.* ALICE *smiles at him.* RACHEL *looks at* ALICE. ALICE *doesn't know what to say.*

ALICE (*gesturing the vodka bottle*). Can I borrow that?

RACHEL. Yeah.

> ALICE *takes a swig.* PETER *stands up and tucks an errant bit of sheet in, with a complicated smile.*

ALICE. Suzy and Mike have finally got together –

RACHEL. Have they?

ALICE. Yeah.

RACHEL. I don't really know Suzy that well…

ALICE. Oh, she's great, I should introduce you –

RACHEL. Yeah, I've met her.

ALICE. No. I mean, you should, you should definitely come out with us some time –

RACHEL. Okay.

PETER. Girls' night out? You should definitely do that.

ALICE (*swinging a grateful grin in* PETER*'s direction*). So you'll come?

RACHEL. Okay.

ALICE. Brilliant.

JAMES. This is a shit music collection, you know –

PETER. James –

RACHEL. Yeah, I know.

JAMES. Pete, take an interest, mate, sort your girlfriend's music collection out.

RACHEL. Yeah.

JAMES. No, I'm not being serious. Your mum's really lovely, by the way, she tried to invite us to dinner –

RACHEL. Did she?

JAMES. Yeah.

Beat. JAMES *tries to touch* ALICE *surreptitiously.* RACHEL *notices.* ALICE *notices* RACHEL *notice and steps away from her boyfriend's grasp.*

Pause. RACHEL *smiles. She looks at* ALICE *directly.* JAMES *notices and takes a step away from* ALICE, *and then, because he doesn't want it to look obvious, he takes another step, and then he walks to the other side of the room.*

This is nice, this room –

ALICE. This is really nice actually –

JAMES (*turning to his girlfriend, all hips*). Which is different from nice how?

ALICE. What?

PETER. By being 'really nice' I think, mate…

JAMES (*small exclusive chuckle*). Okay.

ALICE. We think Mr Taylor might have been sacked.

RACHEL. Yeah?

JAMES. Well. Yeah. Alice thinks he might have touched up
    Rebecca –

ALICE. She's been telling him about her period.

JAMES. Apparently he's 'really good to talk to'. Which means
    he's a pervert. I mean, she's got nothing even to talk about
    neither – though it could be her period, I suppose, if there's
    some discharge in it – he's a pervert whatever, I think.
    Anyway, he's off at the moment, someone's taking his
    lessons –

PETER (*turning to* RACHEL). Are you okay?

RACHEL (*with a funny face*). Yes.

PETER. It's good, isn't it? Having everyone here –

RACHEL. Is it?

JAMES. Leave her alone, mate…

PETER. What?

JAMES (*to* RACHEL). More vodka?

Beat. He takes the vodka from ALICE, *who lets him, and
gives it to* RACHEL, *who lets him. She wipes the lid and has
a swig.* PETER *then tries to take it from her, and she
reluctantly lets him. He puts it on the chest of drawers, away
from everyone.*

Oh, and Colin Jackson is coming to school, that's the other
thing, to do prize-giving – Nightingale's really excited – it's
really funny actually – he's not Colin Jackson, he's 'World-
Record-Holder Colin Jackson'. He's given an assembly
about you too –

RACHEL. Has he?

JAMES. Yeah.

ALICE. We had a policeman come in and tell us about safety
    and everything –

RACHEL. Who?

PETER *tugs on his asthma inhaler. He looks around to see if anyone's watching him.* JAMES *moves over towards the vodka.*

ALICE. The policeman?

RACHEL. Yeah.

ALICE. I don't know.

RACHEL. Okay.

PETER. I wasn't there, it was just for the girls…

Beat. ALICE *walks over to where* JAMES *is, just because she wants to stand close to him.* JAMES *picks up a hairclip from the top of* RACHEL*'s chest of drawers, studiously avoiding the vodka. He puts the hairclip down again. He fiddles with one of the drawer knobs, but he doesn't open anything.*

JAMES. Everyone's been talking about you…

RACHEL. Saying what?

ALICE. Just loads of nice stuff.

JAMES. Pretending you're their best friend. It was getting boring… I mean, it's stopped now basically…

RACHEL. Yeah?

JAMES. Everyone's been really dumb about it.

RACHEL. Yeah.

Pause. ALICE *takes* JAMES*'s hand.* PETER *moves closer to* RACHEL.

JAMES. Has the police said anything?

Beat.

RACHEL. No. Not much. I'm just – we did… a photofit.

JAMES. How come they aren't showing that around the school then?

RACHEL. I don't know.

JAMES. Probably just want to catch him, that's what's wrong with the whole thing actually. They should be showing us and saying, 'Fuck catching him, let's just prevent this happening to more girls.' Shouldn't they?

RACHEL. I don't know.

JAMES. Not my problem, I suppose. How come you don't have a TV up here?

RACHEL. I didn't want one.

JAMES. So what do you do? When Peter's not here –

RACHEL. Oh. I can't remember.

Beat.

ALICE. Okay.

Beat. PETER *wakes up and moves half a step closer to* RACHEL, *both* JAMES *and* ALICE *watch him. Then* RACHEL'*s mobile phone goes off. She picks it up and rejects the call.*

PETER. Who was it?

RACHEL. I didn't know the number...

PETER. It could have been the police...

RACHEL. No.

JAMES. Listen to him! All responsible now, are you, Petey? Peter told you about county trials... Baylis thinks he's a shoo-in...

PETER. No. I'm not –

JAMES. He couldn't get picked for the school team before this year. I think he did a soccer-skills thing during the summer and never told anyone –

RACHEL (*to* PETER). You didn't tell me – That's good, isn't it?

JAMES. Yeah. It is.

PETER. It doesn't mean anything.

JAMES. You watch him. He'll get the lead in the musical next –

ALICE (*giggle*). We watched them do the auditions, you could just sit there if you were auditioning too, so we just sat there…

PETER. You auditioned?

JAMES. No, mate, you go for it. It was funny watching though – (*Sings*.) 'Maybe this time…'

ALICE. It was pathetic.

JAMES *checks his watch*, RACHEL *notices him. He notices* RACHEL *noticing him and blushes*.

RACHEL. You better go. I'm pretty tired.

PETER. Yeah. She's pretty tired.

Beat. JAMES *shrinks slightly.* ALICE *dwindles too.* RACHEL, *annoyed with* PETER, *tries to help them.*

RACHEL. Going somewhere nice?

ALICE. No. Everyone's just meeting at The Dog and Goat.

RACHEL. Are you going, Peter?

PETER. No.

JAMES. Aren't you? Okay.

Pause.

ALICE. Are you two closer? Would you say? Now this has all happened? I mean, me and Jay got closer just because when he got ill, I went round there a lot. But that wasn't a proper illness…

RACHEL. Yeah?

Pause.

JAMES. We got closer because she let me shag her but she won't say that –

ALICE (*giggles*). Shut up.

Pause. JAMES *moves closer to* ALICE, ALICE *sways towards him.*

JAMES. There's nothing we can do, by the way? Like, you want lifting or anything…

Pause. RACHEL *looks at* PETER *accusingly.*

RACHEL. Where?

JAMES (*looking at* PETER *too. Laughs*). I don't know.

Pause.

PETER. I think everything's fine, isn't it?

RACHEL. Is it?

JAMES (*laying it on thick*). Is it?

PETER. Yeah. I mean, I don't know.

RACHEL. Yeah. It's fine.

PETER. Okay.

Blackout.

1.3

24th January.

PETER *is sitting, watching* RACHEL *sleep. He doesn't move a muscle. He just sits in his seat and watches her. It's dark, we can barely see anything.*

ANGELA *enters ever so quietly.*

ANGELA. She asleep?

PETER. Yeah.

ANGELA *moves to the bed and sits gently beside her daughter. She traces her daughter's outline with her hand. But she never touches her.* PETER *just watches, unsure what to do.*

ANGELA. How is she?

PETER. Yeah. Okay.

ANGELA. You're speaking quite loudly, Peter –

Beat. PETER *lowers his head slightly.*

(*Trying to correct herself.*) Arsched says this is all perfectly normal –

PETER. Yeah?

Pause. She silently pulls up a chair and sits beside him.

ANGELA. You know better than any of us really…

PETER. Yeah?

ANGELA. Well, that's a good thing, isn't it? Will you call me Angela, Peter?

PETER. What? Okay.

ANGELA. They all call, and she says she won't have them. All her other friends…

PETER. Yeah?

ANGELA (*gets up from her chair*). Have the police spoken to you?

PETER. No.

ANGELA. I keep phoning them up. I imagine it's really very annoying for them. Rachel doesn't seem that… worried. Still, I suppose that's perfectly natural. She doesn't want me involved. Social services sit with her whenever they come. Arsched says it'll all be okay with that. The police are very kind about it too. I just want him caught, you know.

Pause. ANGELA *circles* RACHEL *slightly, she's now closer to* PETER.

Now. (*Small presumptive sniff.*) Do you… kiss… still?

PETER. What?

ANGELA. I, uh, it's not my business, but I still want her to still be normal… with you… I know she's making you do… you're having to nurse her. You're doing brilliantly.

PETER. Yeah?

ANGELA. Arsched tells me to respect what she wants. But I know I should be up here.

PETER. I'm not, really. I mean, we're pretty normal...

ANGELA (*quiet*). Will you try and get her to talk to me?

PETER. Yeah? I think, I mean, I don't want to upset her...

ANGELA. Okay.

PETER. Sorry. I mean, yeah...

Beat.

ANGELA. It is quite... strange... isn't it – why she wants you here?

PETER. Yeah?

ANGELA. They tell me she can't move her legs because she's afraid of her... vagina. Of the whole... sex, of her sex. And if that's true then why does she want her boyfriend here? I think you're doing brilliantly though... you really are...

ANGELA *gets up and walks to the door.* PETER *takes a tug on his inhaler. The lights start to slowly fade.*

(*Speaks so quietly it's difficult to make out what she says.*) You're right, I don't want her getting upset, if she wakes up... finds me...

PETER. No. I didn't mean that.

ANGELA. No... you're right.

Pause. She's finding it really difficult to leave. PETER *looks round at her.*

I sometimes think we should force her – just tell her they can work – because they can – medically – but then they tell me that this is medical too – her thinking her leg's dead is somehow... medical...

PETER. She's going to get better.

ANGELA. I know…

PETER. No. I mean, you've, uh… I'm going to try really hard…

ANGELA. Okay. Well. Come down when you're ready.

PETER. I'm going to make sure she gets better. I know what I'm doing. Really…

ANGELA. Okay. I'll cook you something if you like.

The lights are in blackout. ANGELA *exits.*

PETER. Okay.

ACT TWO

2.1

30th January.

The lights ping on, full beam. The scene change is instant (there is nothing to change, though perhaps RACHEL*'s duvet has been pulled up over her feet – just slightly).* PETER *is standing where the previous scene left him.*

RACHEL (*soft, she can't get enough liquid in her mouth, every time she opens her mouth we can hear it – a soft shtick on every word*). He had a knife, he said, I didn't see that till – he just told me, I didn't see it till later. And he just stood in the… path, and he said about the knife, and then 'You've got to follow me.' Polite and everything, very… honest. He said I had to follow him. That he wasn't… He wasn't going to be behind me, he was going to be in front of me and that I had to follow him. So I did, he was maybe three or four steps in front and I was just – following – and we came to this small – there was some swings and some – this big – and he took me to basically a shed, I followed him, to, I don't know, a shed, basically, I mean, probably the allotments, but not, definite, and he turned a light on, it was this – bulb – and then, like, undress…

Pause. She paddles backwards with her shoulder, she turns as if to look at him. He turns towards her too. But they don't quite make it. She paddles with her shoulder again.

(*Her voice is full of snot.*) And then he, uh – (*Clears her throat, it doesn't work; clears her throat again.*) I wish I could – I can't even see the inside of… it. I mean, it could be a shed or a… It could have be… They can't even find it.

Pause. Both of them keep very still now, as if being judged.

PETER (*soft, flicking himself out of the softness*). You don't have to – tell me…

RACHEL. I had to stand in there – I had to be slow, taking off the clothes, I can't remember how he said it, but he told me which bits he wanted off first... He spoke really detailed...

Beat.

He said – uh, he wanted my T-shirt off – saying how he wished it was a shirt, he liked buttons... How can I remember this and not the – shed? And then he wouldn't let me take off my underwear for ages because he said he liked that. He kept telling me what he liked. And I threw up sometimes and he made me clean it up with my T-shirt. He tried to do it through my knickers because – and then he asked if it was my first time, saying he was pleased it was him because he could – appreciate it. And he put his fingers all over me, I remember these... They were so scratchy, like, old skin and, he never used his nails.

Pause. She looks up at him, frightened. He takes a tug on his inhaler, she watches him.

Do you want to know the worst bit? Do – you – that sounds such a – but... (*Giggle.*) The worst bit was – was when the doctors examined me afterwards, because then I felt it... all. They put me in this room, they call it a suite but it's a room – the police – and then the doctors come and... They had to – take samples from me – my – me – vagina, my... bum, my mouth, my – they had to take cuttings of my pube... And the doctor had this latex, his breath smelt of latex too – or rubber or whatever it is – like an uncle with his face up close... It felt like the dentist. It was then... after... that I couldn't get off the table, they couldn't get me off. It was then my legs didn't work. And he just smiled and then frowned. And there was this woman, police officer, and she was just sitting there watching it as if he was normal. And that was the... Is that terrible? That that's the... That I think that?

Beat.

Peter?

PETER. I don't... Have you got – is there anything I can ask?

RACHEL. What?

PETER. For – the – is there anything you'd like me to ask? Anything you want me to know but want me to ask the questions for?

RACHEL. What?

PETER. It just feels like you want me to ask something…

RACHEL. No –

PETER. It sounded as if you weren't saying something.

RACHEL. I said everything.

She reaches out a hand to him, but he doesn't meet it. So she turns it into a hand reaching for a cup, she drains it. He walks to the foot of her bed, and pulls the duvet over her toes, before coming back up the bed to stand beside her.

PETER. Shall I get some more water?

Pause. She looks at him carefully.

I'm really pleased you told me. I think it's important. Yeah.

RACHEL. He, uh, he helped me clean up afterwards. He found some – cloth – my T-shirt or… I don't know. I couldn't even feel it but he – I couldn't stop bleeding and he… And then I said that I wouldn't tell anyone, I said I didn't want him to tell anyone, that was so he could believe the lie. Because it was shameful, I said. Because I thought he could kill me otherwise. An' then he took the knife and he said 'Just as a reminder'…

PETER. My / mum…

RACHEL. I told him he had to help me by keeping it a secret, I had blood on my face, and he said he would and he sort of – patted – the side of my – face… and then he started punching where he'd cut, to make sure it scarred, he said… just punching… but the doctors say it'll be okay… and he didn't break anything…

Beat.

PETER. Do you want to... talk... I mean, it must have been pretty bad, so we could – we could talk about this stuff. Just talk it out.

RACHEL. Okay. Aren't we doing that?

PETER. No. Listen, I've been thinking about – I was thinking I should like sit in on your sessions with Arsched – I want to be part of making you better...

RACHEL. Why?

PETER. I just mean, well, I'm here, aren't I?

RACHEL. I know...

PETER. No, I just think I should come along, it's only fair...

RACHEL. Fair?

PETER. No, I mean, really help you. With the police too, I mean, you've told me everything so I could come to that. I know now, I won't judge, I can be a better support than all of them. I mean, it must be hard you saying it all the time and you know that I won't – that I know it now so I could be there – to support you...

RACHEL (*quiet*). But I don't want that.

PETER. It's just that when Mum got sick – I used to go to the therapist's and everything with her all the time. Sometimes they'd talk alone but mostly I'd go in with her – and I was only eight or something then... Just sitting in, you know.

Pause. She picks up a hairbrush from beside her bed and begins to brush her hair. He watches her carefully.

That's why I think I could be helping more... with you...

Pause.

RACHEL. Arsched told me, I'd decided you were safe... I don't know why I did that... sexually, I mean, safe. He reckons I can't move my legs because I said in my head I wanted to be safe from sex. He said I must have decided you were safe too... sexually...

Beat.

PETER. I talked to Alice actually, and she – before, I haven't told her the stuff that – I mean, she's great to talk to – I mean, I just think talking it out helps, I think I could really help…

RACHEL. What did you say to her?

PETER. I don't know. I didn't know most of the stuff, did I? Just, I don't know, how I was feeling… I don't know. I mean –

RACHEL. I'm not jealous, Peter. I don't think you're her type –

PETER. No… Look, she really likes you – she said how much she liked you, when she, uh –

RACHEL. Peter, that's just something someone like her would say –

Pause. PETER *shifts his chair forward, it makes a funny noise, he looks down to where the noise is coming from, he can't work it out.*

PETER. Well, that's not important – I want to be involved, that's all I'm saying, I'd be really good at helping you, I could really support you. (*Spilling.*) Rachel, what happened – with the – I know we didn't talk about it – but I don't want you to worry about that. I can control that.

RACHEL. What?

PETER. I just was lying really close to you – and you're really pretty – it won't happen again.

RACHEL. It doesn't matter.

PETER. It won't happen again, I know what I'm doing, just – let me be part of it…

Knock on the door.

ANGELA. Kids?

RACHEL. Mum…

ANGELA (*opening the door*). Hi. Is this okay?

RACHEL. No.

ANGELA. I've got your washing –

> RACHEL *says nothing.* ANGELA *carries the basket of washing over to* RACHEL*'s chest of drawers.*

> So what have you two been up to –

RACHEL. Peter can put that away...

ANGELA. I'm sure Peter doesn't want to put your underwear away for you...

PETER. I don't mind.

> *Beat.*

ANGELA. Hello, Peter.

PETER. Hi. Do you want me to –

RACHEL. See? He can do it.

> *Pause.* ANGELA *puts the basket down on top of the chest of drawers.*

ANGELA. I can't just sit downstairs –

RACHEL (*exploding*). SO GET YOUR OWN LIFE!

ANGELA. Rachel –

RACHEL. WHAT?

> *Pause.* ANGELA *thinks a moment, and then leaves.*

ANGELA. I'll see you downstairs, Peter...

RACHEL. Will you?

> *Pause.* RACHEL *listens for the footsteps going down the stairs.*

> She's so... big, all the time... and then being so 'I'll see you downstairs, Peter' making herself sound big... You better go.

PETER. What?

RACHEL. I want to be on my own for a little bit.

PETER. Why?

Pause. He walks over to her chest of drawers and starts looking at unpacking the laundry. He picks up a pair of knickers.

RACHEL. I mean it, Peter…

He puts down the pair of knickers.

PETER. But I want to stay up here…

RACHEL. Well, I can't leave, can I?

PETER. What?

RACHEL (*mimicking*). 'What?'

Pause.

PETER. I just think you're being unfair, to me, to Angela…

RACHEL. 'Angela'?

PETER. What? Listen. As long as I haven't done anything wrong…

RACHEL. 'Angela'?

Pause. She touches her scar.

PETER. Look, today was a good day, okay? Let's not ruin things by fighting about things that aren't really important – I think – I'm going to stay for a bit…

Pause. She pushes her arm under her pillow.

Are you okay then?

Blackout.

2.2

2nd February.

ALICE *is sitting in the room. She's a bit fidgety and entirely different without* JAMES *to chaperone her speaking.*

ALICE. But then we talked all about that, and he didn't even like that, he thought I liked it, which is why he invited me. Or he said that, I'm not sure if I believe him really –

RACHEL. Okay.

ALICE. He could be lying because he doesn't want us to split up, so he wants to pretend there isn't a problem. Anyway, we're going to try spending more time together –

Pause.

Your face is healing well, isn't it?

RACHEL (*wants to touch her scar, but doesn't*). Yeah.

ALICE. Do you want me to bring some make-up? Cover-stick, that sort of thing…

RACHEL. No.

ALICE. My mum said she wanted to buy a present for you, when she heard about it, so I could get her to pay.

RACHEL. No. Is Peter okay? At school?

ALICE. Yeah, he's great. Everyone's treating him a bit like – like he's special, because of what happened and because he's being, you know, so supportive for you. I mean, he is special, isn't he? He was brilliant to talk to about the whole James thing – I mean, because he understands what James is really like, you know –

RACHEL. Yeah.

ALICE. I mean, they're not getting on great at the moment, but they've been friends for so long, I mean, far longer than either of us have been around – with them –

RACHEL. Yeah.

ALICE. So they'll be friends again, though my mum said, when I talked to her about it, that she doesn't really know that many friends from school, which I found really weird. It'll be quite funny really if we stop being friends and then we meet up again later, at a reunion or whatever. Though she said she hadn't had any school reunions either. We've got to have a school reunion, I think. In ten years or whatever, I mean… I mean, my mum isn't even bothering with the website thing or anything like that, but I'd *love* to know what everyone's doing in ten years, it'd be so interesting…

RACHEL. Yeah.

ALICE. You think so?

RACHEL. Is Peter the same though – as he was?

ALICE. Yeah, I mean, everyone's really giving him respect. I mean, I'm sure he'd like it better if you were around, but you still get to see each other loads, don't you?

RACHEL. Not the way we were… no.

ALICE. Does it seem really long ago now?

RACHEL. What?

ALICE. Well, when it all started –

RACHEL. When I was… attacked?

ALICE. Yeah.

RACHEL. No.

ALICE. It seems really long ago to me –

RACHEL. Does it?

ALICE. I suppose you've been here mostly. But Peter said you might come down for the trials –

RACHEL. Did he?

ALICE. Yeah. James is going now, having a go now, so I'm going to go too. Did you hear about all that?

RACHEL. What?

ALICE. Mr Baylis was a wanker and said that he shouldn't do the trials, but James thought about it and said he was at least as good as the other players going, and it's open trials anyway, it's not even proper. Did Peter tell you about that?

RACHEL. No.

ALICE. I think he's pleased, that James is going –

RACHEL. Probably.

ALICE. I thought about not going – because of what we decided – about me not having to be with him all the time – doing girls' nights and stuff like that – which you have to come to, by the way – and then I thought that I'd actually quite like to see the trials – because when stuff like that's important, you know – I mean, you're going even and you're basically here most of the time –

RACHEL. If I'm better –

ALICE. Really? Oh, Peter said it like it was definite. He said you were getting so much better so quickly. He said he could almost see it – how much better you were getting. Or that may be me thinking that, and he didn't say that at all. I don't think Peter says things like that – but he definitely said you were getting tonnes better. Well. It doesn't matter. It's funny, isn't it? How we never used to be friends – I mean, even with James and Peter being –

RACHEL. We don't need to be friends.

Pause.

ALICE. Are you seeing a psychiatrist?

RACHEL. Psychologist.

ALICE. I had a feeling about that. What's that like? That's not rude, is it – it's just I knew a girl – who had to use one. A cousin of my mum's. She fell in love with hers.

RACHEL. Arsched's fifty.

ALICE (*laugh*). Oh. Okay. Oh, I'm doing the musical *Cabaret*. I got a part.

RACHEL. Did you?

ALICE. Yeah, weird, isn't it?

RACHEL. No.

ALICE. I just went afterwards... don't tell James... It's not a big part... well, it's quite big.

RACHEL. Okay.

ALICE. He's waiting downstairs, by the way. Do you want him to come up?

RACHEL. Who?

ALICE. James. Just don't tell him about the musical.

RACHEL. He's downstairs...

ALICE. Don't worry, he won't come up...

RACHEL. What?

ALICE. Or I could go? You know, if you're bored or anything, I don't mind – It's weird, isn't it? Because basically I only normally see you with James and Peter – He's really sweet, you know, James –

RACHEL. Yeah.

ALICE. I know you don't like him but I think the four of us could be really good friends, it's just you've got to catch him when he's being funny. I mean, he likes you, he thinks you're really nice –

RACHEL. When did you lose... your virginity?

ALICE. Oh.

RACHEL. It's just – I know I was later than everyone else...

ALICE. Not that later – I mean... Everyone lies about that stuff, don't they? I know Michelle Milsom didn't lose hers at fourteen and she says she did.

RACHEL. I hadn't – before the...

ALICE. Oh.

RACHEL. Yeah. I suppose, at least it's over with...

ALICE. It feels odd, doesn't it? I mean, obviously it was different and everything...

RACHEL. Yeah, it is.

Beat.

ALICE. Can I do anything?

RACHEL. What?

ALICE. No. It doesn't matter.

Pause. JAMES appears in the doorway, neither of them notice him.

JAMES. Your mum wanted to ask if we wanted dinner, she's going to cook... But I said we probably should go... Hi. Rachel. I mean – do you want to go straight away or, you know, I could chat a bit...

RACHEL. Hi.

JAMES. Yeah. Peter said you just wanted to chat to Alice really...

ALICE. No. He just said you wanted to talk to a girl...

RACHEL. Did he?

JAMES. Yeah. I got that actually – I mean, Peter probably talks about the same stuff I do. I mean, you and Alice have probably got more in common.

ALICE. Yeah.

Pause. RACHEL squeezes her head around to look at ALICE.

RACHEL. He asked you to come?

ALICE. I wanted to – and then he said you could do with talking to a girl, and I thought that was – brilliant. Though James wasn't supposed to come up...

JAMES. I'm allowed to come up!

RACHEL. He shouldn't have asked you.

ALICE. I was really pleased though.

Pause.

JAMES. He's not about then?

RACHEL. No. He's doing some football thing…

JAMES. Is he?

RACHEL. Yeah. I mean… That's what he said…

JAMES (*laugh*). Well, it's not another girl…

RACHEL. Yeah, I know…

JAMES. He's probably getting you a present or something. (*Laugh.*) Or doing the football thing, of course…

RACHEL. Yeah.

JAMES. It's probably a football thing. I just hadn't heard about it.

RACHEL. Yeah.

JAMES. Did he… get picked?

RACHEL. For what?

JAMES. Okay. Doesn't matter…

RACHEL. Okay.

Pause.

JAMES. He's doing alright, though, with you? Being supportive and everything?

RACHEL. Yeah.

JAMES. Good. I was a bit worried he was going to be a wanker.

Blackout.

2.3

7th February.

RACHEL *is asleep.* ANGELA *is sitting beside her.* PETER
enters with two cups of tea, one of which he puts beside
ANGELA*'s chair, on the floor. He has to bend down far too far to*
get it there, making a hugely concerted effort not to spill
anything, whilst still holding the other cup, it looks quite comical.

ANGELA. Thanks, love.

Pause. PETER *sits down.*

PETER. Is she… uh?

ANGELA (*can't take her eyes off her daughter*). Her dad
always used to let her fall asleep on the sofa. Watching the
TV, sometimes, not all the time. He only did it because he
liked carrying her upstairs to bed.

PETER. Yeah?

ANGELA. They looked very… gentle together…

PETER. I wish I'd met him…

ANGELA. Don't – there's something about remembering that
always makes you remember it better. I remember – after
Ian… died – I wrote a note to myself saying don't think he
was brilliant –

PETER. Yeah?

ANGELA. You've got to remember that, otherwise you didn't
love them. It must be the same with you and Rachel, you
might only remember how great it was before… well.
Whatever it was before… But you certainly seemed – I
thought you were a good boyfriend.

PETER. Okay.

ANGELA. I phoned your mum, to say how great you're being,
to check you're okay at home, because this must be difficult
for you. Well, just so she knows…

PETER. Yeah, she said. You didn't need to do that…

ANGELA. She seemed pleased.

PETER. She was okay?

ANGELA. Yeah.

PETER. Okay, I thought she'd been rude.

ANGELA. No, very pleasant.

PETER. She sounded like she'd been rude, when she told me about it.

ANGELA. No. She's had some difficult times... from what Rachel told me. Not much, obviously.

PETER. Not that difficult.

Pause.

I phoned the police...

ANGELA. Did you?

PETER. To ask if I could help. They said no.

ANGELA. Okay.

PETER. Yeah, I mean, they said it was going fine.

ANGELA. It's not.

PETER. Well, I'm not sure you know that...

ANGELA. Sorry?

PETER. I think we're – me and Rachel are doing well – I mean, making progress –

ANGELA. Good, I hope I'm part of it too –

PETER. Yeah, but I'm pretty sure we're on the right track –
I mean, me and Rachel have been talking quite seriously –
I really feel we're getting somewhere – I mean, don't get any hopes up – but, you know, it's a start.

ANGELA. Good. That's – What have you been talking about?

PETER. There is something – I mean, you do come up quite a lot, and I think that's part of the problem you two are having –

ANGELA. You think I'm seeing too much of my daughter?

PETER. No. That doesn't matter that much. I suppose I'm just feeling very confident about it really – you know, I feel great about it really… I think I'm really helping – I'm, um, yeah.

ANGELA. Well. That's great.

RACHEL. I'm not asleep.

Beat.

ANGELA. Did we wake you, love?

RACHEL. No.

Pause.

ANGELA. Do you want me to go?

RACHEL. Put on the light.

PETER *puts the bedside lamp on.*

PETER. Hi.

Pause. RACHEL'*s face adjusts to the light.*

RACHEL. Do you do this every night?

ANGELA. No.

RACHEL. This isn't a hospital. You shouldn't do that.

ANGELA. Okay.

RACHEL. I mean it…

ANGELA. Okay.

Pause. RACHEL *touches her scar, as if to reaffirm it's still there.*

RACHEL (*soft*). What were you saying… about Dad?

ANGELA. Oh. That. Well, I don't know if you remember him, carrying you up to bed.

RACHEL. I remember the game we used to do – 'Sack of Potatoes'.

ANGELA. Yes. That's right. He would get you in your sleeping
bag –

RACHEL. No, he'd put me in there and then he'd put me on his
back, in the bag, and go running around the room, bouncing
me off anything and then he'd put real salt in the bag and
shake it, and then he'd do this thing where he'd pretend he
didn't even like potatoes, so he'd tickle me.

PETER. Yeah?

RACHEL. He used to do an accent…

ANGELA. I did it too…

RACHEL. Okay. Do it now.

ANGELA. I can't remember how it goes.

RACHEL. I think Peter thinks it was better that Dad died.
Because his didn't, his just fucked off.

PETER. No.

Pause.

ANGELA. Are you okay?

RACHEL. I don't even like *him* when you're here…
I remember you, before, and you were so not like any of
this… You were just much better before you became such a
wanker.

ANGELA. Rachel…

RACHEL. Don't pretend you're not pleased, Mum, you've got
no reason to be jealous now. He's just as crap as you are.

ANGELA. Rachel, don't be silly. I don't understand what
you're saying.

RACHEL. I knew you were the worst one before, Mum, and
now I'm not so sure. Listen to him.

PETER. I wasn't saying anything…

RACHEL. I'VE BEEN LISTENING TO YOU! I listened to
you. You were telling her all you'd done for me, like it was
some kind of an achievement.

ANGELA. It is, if you're getting better –

RACHEL. BUT I'M NOT! Am I? Where are my fucking legs if I am getting better?

ANGELA. Rachel, it'll take time. Be fair.

RACHEL. NEITHER OF YOU ARE DOING ANYTHING!

ANGELA. I'd like to –

RACHEL. BUT YOU'RE FUCKING TALKING! I should go to sleep now…

Pause.

ANGELA. Perhaps that is for the best.

PETER. Yeah.

RACHEL (*dangerous*). What?

Pause.

ANGELA. Do you want that light still on?

RACHEL. I can turn it off…

ANGELA. Sure?

RACHEL (*demonstrates*). My hand can reach, thanks…

ANGELA. I don't even know what we've done…

Pause. ANGELA *exits,* PETER *follows her.*

PETER (*to* RACHEL). Bye.

ANGELA (*to* RACHEL). I love you.

RACHEL *looks to where her mum just left, and then turns off the light.*

Pause. She shifts and looks in the opposite direction.

She reaches a hand back and turns the light on again. She keeps staring away from the door.

Blackout.

ACT THREE

3.1

11th February.

PETER *puts his arms around* RACHEL *and pulls her up the bed. This is something they've done thousands of times now. She gets there and takes a breath and so does he.*

RACHEL. I wanted to be a nurse once.

PETER. Did you?

RACHEL. It was when I decided all jobs were selfish, because my mum was switching. I wanted to be a nurse or a police officer because they'd be the jobs I didn't want to do ever.

PETER. Really?

Pause.

(*Appraises what he is going to do.*) If we, um, twist you round, so that you'll be leaning against the – bedhead and then we put your feet on the ground. It's okay…

RACHEL. If it hurts, I want you to keep going anyway.

PETER. Okay.

Pause. A moment's indecision, and then he gets to work. He twists her around, he puts her feet so they can touch the ground. This leaves her with her body cuddling up against the headboard of the bed. Her feet are floppy and useless, her back is twisted.

I wanted to be a politician.

RACHEL. What?

PETER. Yeah, I know. But my mum kept this badge I had made. I found it, recently, I mean, really recently – I was going to bring it in for you to look at.

RACHEL. But you changed your mind –

PETER. Yeah, I decided against it, I don't know why – I don't know, it's just a badge –

RACHEL. Who were you standing for? On the badge?

PETER (*throat laugh*). The Peter Party.

RACHEL. Really?

PETER. That's what the badge said –

RACHEL (*giggle*). What were your policies?

PETER. I don't think I had those. I think it was just 'vote for me, I'll make all the decisions when I have to', I think I mainly liked how the politicians dressed… The suits, you know…

RACHEL (*giggle*). Brilliant.

Pause. He sizes her up.

(*Looking at his anxiety.*) I think you should just keep going.

PETER. Okay.

PETER *faces her like a weightlifter, full-on and strong, he pulls her hard up by her armpits, her feet are like puppets' feet, they don't find ground.*

(*Full of strain.*) Uh –

He lets her back down again, he has to try hard to not let his momentum cause him to fall into her. She tries to remain sitting, she doesn't want to go back to lying down. But this means as soon as he gets her down, she starts slipping off the bed, she can't get hold of enough of her headboard. She can't use her feet to arrest her ascent, and her back is exhausted, she makes a small squeak from her mouth as she slips.

PETER *catches her, or half-catches her, and part of her stays on the bed, and slowly, inch by inch, she regains balance and she's sitting again. Or grasping onto the headboard anyway.*

Pause. They both try and regain sense.

Pause. PETER *takes a tug on his inhaler.*

RACHEL. Okay. Again?

PETER. Um –

RACHEL. If you're – we should –

PETER. Really?

RACHEL. Yeah.

PETER. Okay.

He heaves her up by her armpits and takes the full weight of her on his body. His body isn't vertical, it's half-vertical, with his arse sticking out almost as a ballast. He grabs her around the waist, they're stuck in a horrible position. She is standing against him, she is totally leaning on him, but she's upright. This is an enormous strain for both of them. Her legs don't work to any degree.

(*Everything about him is strained.*) Okay?

RACHEL. Yeah.

PETER. Sure?

RACHEL (*trying not to cry*). Yeah.

PETER. You think… can you try… standing…

RACHEL. No.

PETER. Okay, time to get down…

He starts to waddle her back to the bed. He's using all his strength to lift her. But he can't move her far enough or fast enough. In a series of disjointed manoeuvres he puts her down on the floor. She makes another squeaking noise as he does. They haven't made it back to the bed. She lies on the floor, he hovers somewhere close.

(*Desperately out of breath.*) Sorry.

RACHEL (*exhausted too*). Okay.

He takes a squirt on his inhaler.

No rush, we can stay like this, I like it here…

PETER *coughs, he's exhausted. Pause.*

Can I lie in your lap? To get my head up…

PETER. Yeah?

RACHEL. Okay?

He changes to a sitting position, and helps her put her head on his lap, he leans against the wall. Finally, they've found a comfortable pose, and they both relax as they realise that fact. They look nice together. PETER *coughs again and touches his chest where it hurts, but then he smiles.*

Can you reach my knee?

PETER. Yeah.

RACHEL. Will you pinch it? Don't say when?

She covers her face with her hands. PETER *is slightly surprised. He thinks and then he moves to tweak her knee cautiously.*

(*As he hovers his hand above, he doesn't make it.*) Then?

PETER. No.

RACHEL. Try again…

PETER *moves quickly and tweaks her knee.*

I could feel your arm move…

PETER. Okay.

Pause. She slumps into his lap.

RACHEL. I think we should go on a date.

PETER. What?

RACHEL. Just to the cinema, or ice-skating, or dinner. Or a boat trip, just a canoe or… Somewhere nice, I think you should start saving up for it now. Sell all the boxes of chocolates people have sent me.

PETER. Okay.

RACHEL. Yeah? Just somewhere nice, it doesn't have to be expensive, and I mean that – about the chocolates –

PETER. I think your mum will pay actually, she keeps trying to thrust money down my throat –

RACHEL (*keeping positive*). Okay.

PETER. Yeah.

RACHEL. When we got together – did you think we'd last?

PETER. Yeah.

RACHEL. Good.

PETER. Yeah, I mean, how long?

RACHEL. How long did you think?

PETER. I was really chuffed when it happened though – I mean, you're really pretty. You still are.

She reaches her hand up past her scar, towards his throat.

RACHEL. Bring your – I want to touch your face…

He bullet-laughs.

I do. Can I?

PETER. Yeah.

He moves his face down, she gently manipulates her hands over it.

RACHEL (*moves her hands down over his shoulders, rubbing them*). Do you like this?

PETER. Yeah.

Pause. She smiles at him strangely.

(*Hmmph-laugh.*) What?

RACHEL. Bring your head down. Please. Peter.

PETER. I'm really sweaty…

He does, she holds onto his head with the back of her hand, again he's stuck in an odd position, their faces close together.

Pause. She takes his hand.

RACHEL. Smile.

    PETER *does*.

    Bring your face in, I wanted to see your smile really closer.
Over my eyes. I want to smell your breath –

PETER (*trying to withdraw*). No.

RACHEL (*keeping him held in*). Come on...

PETER. No.

RACHEL (*trying to pull his head down even closer*). Come on...

PETER (*really struggling quite hard*). Please. Ow!

RACHEL (*trying to pull her face up to meet his*). Come on...

PETER (*forcibly dislocates her*). What's the *matter* with you...

    Pause.

RACHEL. I want you to give me a bed bath –

PETER. What?

RACHEL. I'll tell you what to do.

    Pause.

PETER. I think I should get you back on the bed.

RACHEL. Not yet.

    *Pause. A hoover starts on the stairs. As they talk, it slowly
approaches the door, doing a stair at a time.* RACHEL *acts
like she doesn't notice, but the hoover makes* PETER *even
more nervous*.

    Will you give me a bed bath?

PETER. No. Of course not. Who normally does it? I'll get her.

RACHEL. Why?

    Beat. The hoover is fast approaching.

PETER. The nurse or your mum should do it. Bath you.

RACHEL. I don't want them to.

PETER. When's the nurse next coming?

RACHEL. I don't want her to.

PETER. Then why do you want me to?

RACHEL. Because you're my boyfriend.

Pause. PETER *half-stutters out a laugh.*

You don't apologise much any more.

PETER. What?

RACHEL. You don't say sorry much any more.

PETER. Yeah?

RACHEL. Why does no one behave like I want them to...

PETER. I think I do, actually...

RACHEL. You're starting to smell like her too.

PETER. It smells in here actually...

RACHEL. Then give me my bed bath! Do you not want to see me?

Beat. The hoover is getting closer and closer.

You don't want to touch me... see my... see me.

PETER. No, I just think your mum would really like that.

RACHEL. I don't want my mum to perve on me.

Pause. The hoover switches off. RACHEL *smiles at that, and then frowns back at* PETER. *They don't say anything for a bit, and when they do, they speak quietly, as if someone's listening.*

PETER. I should get you back on the bed.

RACHEL. I like it here.

PETER *starts to manipulate her up.* RACHEL *resists as much as she can.*

No, Peter.

PETER (*looking towards the door*). SH!

RACHEL (*pushing his body hard away*). NO!

> *He gives up. He looks carefully at the door. Footsteps are heard going down the stairs.*

PETER (*quiet and vicious*). You just want to stay on the floor?

RACHEL. Yes!

> *Pause.*

It's normal to want to touch me...

PETER (*boiling hot*). I'm just like your mum / anyway...

RACHEL. That's what the problem is?

PETER. You said I was fucking useless...

RACHEL. So give me a bath!

PETER. Why did you say that to her like that?

RACHEL. You care what she thinks?

PETER. WE WERE GETTING BETTER!

RACHEL. WE FUCKING WEREN'T!

PETER. I WAS HELPING YOU!

RACHEL. FUCK OFF!

PETER. Look. *Look*, let's get you *back* on the *bed*...

RACHEL. I don't want that.

> *He starts to lift her.*

I DON'T WANT THAT!

> *She pushes her hand up into his face. He keeps on trying to drag her up. She forces a hand into his eye, all the time wriggling her shoulders away from him.*

PETER. Ow!

> *They size each other up, and then* PETER *tries to lift her again, less apologetically this time, by her shoulders and*

*elbows and whatever else he can manage. She grabs a
handful of his hair, pulls herself up to his level and she half-
headbutts him. They grapple.*

RACHEL (*quiet, concentrated on the effort*). Fucking...

*She manages to hit his head against the side of the bed. Then
she does it again, and it's harder this time. He pushes her
down onto the floor, hard, with the flat of his hand. She bites
his hand, and then tears at his hair and sticks her elbow in
his eye. He hits her down (he doesn't punch, it's with the flat
of his hand – he is determined to use the flat of his hand
wherever possible). She tries to tear at him again, she
scratches his eye.*

PETER. OW!

*She tries to pull at him again. He pushes hard, crack, against
the floor – and holds her there. Pinning her with his weight.*

STOP IT!

*She stops, like a toddler might stop. She doesn't seem to
understand what's going on, she just knows she's been hurt.
He dislocates himself away from her, pulls himself up to
sitting position. She's still lying on the floor. He fiddles in his
pocket and takes another tug on his inhaler. He coughs
repeatedly, and phlegm comes into his mouth, which he then
swallows. She doesn't say anything. It's ages before he
speaks.*

I... just... think it's not good... on the floor.

Pause.

RACHEL. I've worked out – I'd cover everything he could
breathe with – his mouth and – you can do ears too, breathe
through ears too. So I'd – just leave his nose. And then I'd
stand there and I'd just watch him, tied up with tape over his
mouth and his ears and anything he can breathe by. I don't
know whether you can breathe through the eyes – I was quite
surprised about the ear thing. And I'd have a hammer with me,
I'd just sit there mostly, but I'd have a hammer. And every
now and again I'd just tap him, his nose, with the hammer, not
to break it, just to remind him that I had it, and he'd know that

he could only breathe out of his nose, because his mouth and ears are covered, so I'd just keep reminding him of it. And I'd tap it harder and harder but still tapping. Then I'd hit it harder, just so it'd sting or something, just so he really knew. It'd probably be really difficult for him to breathe then, but it'd come back to normal and we'd both wait for that, him and me. Just until it's completely right again. Then I'd break it. He'd probably still be able to breathe then but it'd hurt all the time. Then I'd hit it again until it was flat, his nose, and maybe that'd make him unconscious, the pain, or maybe he'd suffocate. But sometimes I think he's not too bad. I mean, just mixed up a bit, like you. Will you – bring your head down?

Pause.

I think I smell. I can smell myself, Peter. I can smell me, okay? My... I want you to wash me, I want you to see me.

PETER. Anyone can get you clean, if you smell... you don't smell...

Pause. PETER *scratches his hand and touches his eye gingerly. He starts to cry.*

(*Sniff.*) Why... Why did you follow him?

Beat.

No... I'm not accusing, I know there's a reason. If we're being honest.

Pause. PETER *stops crying.*

RACHEL. Will you touch my scar?

PETER (*the phlegm's back in his throat*). What?

RACHEL. To see if it hurts, it doesn't if I touch it, but I can never tell if that means anything...

PETER *bravely reaches out and touches it. She closes her eyes while he does.*

I was raped.

PETER. I know that. Look, I, uh, I think we share this... don't we?

RACHEL. Share what?

PETER. I just think if I don't understand something, I should ask.

RACHEL. Will you go away, Peter?

Beat.

I want you to go.

PETER. Fuck it. Sure.

RACHEL. Yeah?

PETER. You want me to go?

RACHEL. I don't want you to be so fucking gay about it as well.

Pause.

He quivers a moment, and then he leaves.

She listens to him go down the stairs. She tries to count his descent, under her breath.

She finishes counting, she reaches twenty-one, she scratches the top of her arm.

She does nothing.

She hardly moves a muscle, she does nothing, she just lies there.

She counts to twenty-one again.

She gently fiddles with her eye, before reassuming neutral.

She smoothes down her arm.

She thinks. She looks at the side of the bed, and thinks about crawling up it.

She changes her mind, and puts her hand numbly inside her knickers.

She brings it out, checking to see if there's blood on it. There doesn't seem to be.

She smells her hand. She crumples her face as if ready to cry, but she doesn't.

She lies back, she tries to lie back as far as she can. But there isn't far to go.

She smells her hand again. This time there's more efficiency to how she does it.

She looks at her hand and traces the lines on her palm.

She scratches her hair.

She lies and waits.

She just lies there. Perfectly neutral.

An unmoving heavy mass. On the floor. Blackout.

3.2

14th February.

RACHEL *is back in bed and is being helped onto the bedpan by* ANGELA. RACHEL *pushes her knickers down to her mid-thighs, she's getting quite accomplished at this. Again it takes ages for* RACHEL *to start. There is a wheelchair leaning against the wall of the room.*

RACHEL. Ow –

ANGELA *lifts* RACHEL *up some more, to make sure she's firmly over the bedpan.*

ANGELA. When we get the wheelchair working, we'll be able to get you into the toilet.

RACHEL *says nothing.*

I'm your mother. It affects me too… I'm going to keep coming back until you're used to me…

RACHEL. Do you want me to kill myself?

ANGELA (*wiping something away with her shoulder, as she tightens her grip on* RACHEL*'s bum*). I keep thinking I've let you down...

RACHEL. I just don't like you here.

ANGELA. Why? Why can't we talk about this? I want to...

RACHEL. Because I DON'T WANT TO.

ANGELA. Okay.

Pause.

They keep telling me – I phone Arsched – and he says, ask yourself the question 'What can I give this person?' And, uh... that I have to tell you that whatever response you have as a – survivor – is normal and I have to respect that... So I have to just have to be your – I just have to obey you until you change...

RACHEL. Okay.

ANGELA. Rachel, when your dad died...

RACHEL. I don't want to talk about that.

ANGELA. Okay.

Pause.

Okay.

Pause. ANGELA *scratches her ear. Pause.*

Did I do something wrong?

RACHEL. Yes.

ANGELA. When?

RACHEL. The whole thing, okay?

ANGELA. They told me on the phone – they asked me 'Have you ever talked about sex with her?'

RACHEL. No –

ANGELA. It felt like they were accusing – but they said they weren't and I thought all that was done at school now – well,

I know we needed to talk about it, but you were never an easy person to talk to – I mean – but if we had talked about it then it might have meant we could talk about this –

RACHEL. Wait –

Pause.

RACHEL starts to pee. This time the dribble is not so painful. It sounds almost normal.

She farts accidentally. They both keep very still.

They wait for more.

It doesn't come.

ANGELA. I want to talk to you about it, Rachel.

RACHEL (*muffled*). No.

ANGELA. Just tell me what happened.

RACHEL. NO!

ANGELA. Who would do that to a little girl?

RACHEL. I'm not a little girl.

ANGELA. I think –

RACHEL (*turning as far as she can towards her mum*). I DON'T CARE.

Pause. A final dribble, RACHEL makes a slight growling noise, this takes some effort.

ANGELA waits for more, RACHEL concentrates on her bladder.

There's nothing left.

You can go, Mum…

ANGELA. Have you finished?

RACHEL. Yes.

ANGELA. You just wanted a wee, did you…

Beat. RACHEL says nothing.

ANGELA *checks she's steady and then hands her the toilet paper. She attempts to break the paper off for her daughter, but is stopped from doing so.*

RACHEL *uses it aggressively. She dumps the paper in the pan, this causes an involuntary spasm in her back.*

ANGELA *doesn't notice* RACHEL's *pain.*

RACHEL *refocuses on her mother. She pulls up her own knickers.*

RACHEL. I hate you doing this… At least Peter didn't like doing it…

ANGELA. Let's just make this easy…

RACHEL *is helped off the bedpan.* ANGELA *carries it out of the room. Having a quick glance at it as she does.*

RACHEL *waits in silence, she keeps entirely still. She tries not to blink.*

ANGELA *re-enters, she's now washed the bedpan. She puts it back under the bed and picks up* RACHEL's *used dinner tray and carries it out.*

It was nice, that, wasn't it?

RACHEL. If Peter comes back, you're not to say anything, yeah? If he is –

ANGELA. About what?

RACHEL. About anything, Mum. I don't want you to speak to him at all. He's my friend.

ANGELA (*slumping slightly*). Okay.

RACHEL *doesn't say anything, despite* ANGELA's *pathetic eyes. So* ANGELA *exits.*

Nothing. A big crowd of it.

Nothing.

More nothing. RACHEL *tries not to move. She has a system worked out for her first few moments of peace. It's a tried-and-tested system and generally involves anaesthetising herself with great big silences. Blackout.*

3.3

20th February.

ALICE *is sitting there diligently.* RACHEL *has her back turned to her.*

ALICE. Have you been reading anything?

RACHEL. No.

ALICE. We've got this crap book we've got to read for English. What do you do then? Most of your time? Without a TV. I mean, when you're here.

RACHEL. You think I leave at night?

ALICE. What?

RACHEL. What?

 Pause.

 You think I leave at night?

ALICE. Are your feet getting better then?

RACHEL. What?

ALICE. I don't understand.

RACHEL. You said 'when I'm here'.

ALICE. What?

RACHEL. When am I not?

ALICE. No. I just… Have I said something wrong?

 RACHEL *turns over, this takes some effort, to face* ALICE.

 Um. The musical is going well. I've got promoted.

RACHEL. Okay.

ALICE. I still haven't told James though, isn't that pathetic? Still, I've been thinking a lot about that, since we spoke, and we just aren't that kind of couple, you know. I mean, he's amazing in bed. I mean, actually, isn't it funny that that's embarrassing? I mean, it wasn't great to start with but now it's nice – loving, you know. It's funny. I don't know. Have you seen Peter?

RACHEL (*laugh, funny voice*). I thought I left him with you.

ALICE. No. He's not in school. James went to see him, but he wasn't in. His mum was a bitch to James actually. Told him off for leaving his bike on the lawn.

Pause.

Is that a wheelchair?

RACHEL. Yes.

ALICE. Oh. Suzy's split up with –

RACHEL. – I don't know them.

ALICE. Um. I wasn't sure how long to leave it before coming back. I wasn't…

RACHEL. Yeah. What do you want to talk about?

ALICE. There's nothing… I can do or anything…

RACHEL. Do you know why my real friends aren't here? Because they asked, and I said no. They asked me whether I wanted them here, and I didn't…

ALICE. Do you want me to tell them to come over?

RACHEL. Did you not hear what I said?

ALICE. You sounded like you'd changed your mind.

RACHEL. You want to make an announcement in assembly, don't you? 'Rachel's ready to receive visitors she was nasty to before. She's okay now.'

ALICE. No. I just thought you might want someone round here…

RACHEL. Why? To entertain me…

ALICE. Well, it's not exactly entertaining you, is it? It's just chatting really…

RACHEL. Depends how clever you are…

ALICE (*completely crushed – with a big smile*). Have I done something wrong? I mean, I liked it... here...

RACHEL. We don't have anything to talk about...

ALICE. Yeah, but we can talk about loads of stuff, music, things like that...

RACHEL. I don't *like* that stuff...

ALICE. James isn't going to come barging in again. I had such a go at him about that.

Beat.

When you said – about the virginity thing – I wasn't really – when I, it wasn't like he asked or anything. I mean, it wasn't bad or anything like that, but he just didn't really ask. And it is entirely different, I mean, James, I'm in love with him, so when he did it, it was fine. And I didn't say no or anything like that, because it was really surprising, and I had to go and get the twenty-four-hour thing. But it was so weird, you know? I wanted to say, that I wasn't sure when I was going to – I wanted to save it a little bit too. I don't think it's that odd really, wanting to stay a virgin, I mean, I'd have quite liked that. He said afterwards it was an accident, well, he said it like I made a mistake but then we kept doing it after that. Like that had been the first for real rather than an accident.

Pause.

RACHEL. Do you want me to say something?

ALICE. No.

RACHEL. Good.

Pause.

ALICE (*with honour*). You still want me to go?

RACHEL. Yes.

ALICE. Do I come back?

RACHEL. No.

ALICE. Okay.

She picks up her things, she walks out of the room.

Um. I'm not upset. Okay? Don't worry. I'll see you when you're better… Okay? And maybe we can talk. Okay?

ALICE *exits. We hear the clatter of her going down the stairs.* ALICE*'s heels sound more aggressive now.*

RACHEL *sits in silence, she scratches her eyelid.*

Blackout.

3.4

28th February.

ANGELA *has partially lifted up* RACHEL, *and* RACHEL *is also getting leverage by the use of her arms.* ANGELA *is pulling the sheet from under* RACHEL. *This is a complicated but highly efficient procedure.*

RACHEL. Ow –

ANGELA *lifts* RACHEL *up some more, but keeps pulling the sheet.*

That's okay.

ANGELA. Okay.

ANGELA *starts to put a new sheet on the bed. She does so in silence. This is even more of an effort,* RACHEL*'s bum has to be lifted up while the sheet is shunted underneath her.*

RACHEL. Ow.

ANGELA *finishes and starts filling up a washing basket with* RACHEL*'s clothes from the floor.*

ANGELA. You're almost out of knickers.

RACHEL. Because most of those are clean…

ANGELA. What?

RACHEL. You're washing clean knickers.

ANGELA sniffs a pair that she's just put in the basket, the knickers are dirty and smell. She adds them to the basket, while RACHEL giggles. Pause. ANGELA continues putting washing in the basket, as if she hadn't noticed. Then she stops and looks carefully at her daughter.

Pause. RACHEL looks carefully back. She wipes her cheek roughly, she's not crying, but her cheeks are hot. She's melting slightly.

I don't want to be like this…

Beat.

ANGELA (*trying not to rush over*). I know you don't, love…

RACHEL. I… um… I want to be nicer now…

ANGELA. Well, nice isn't so important, but let's get you in the chair, let's be positive…

RACHEL. Not the chair.

ANGELA. The chair will be so useful.

RACHEL. Mum, you're saying the wrong things, okay? I want to be nicer, okay?

Pause.

ANGELA. Okay.

Pause. ANGELA scratches her ear. Pause.

Do you want to talk to me?

RACHEL. Not yet. But I will.

ANGELA. That's good. That's a relief.

RACHEL. Don't cry.

ANGELA. No, I won't. I do love you, you know that?

RACHEL. Yes, I know that.

Pause.

ANGELA. Do you want me to phone any of your friends?

RACHEL. Not yet.

ANGELA. Okay. And we'll try the chair eventually, will we?

RACHEL. I want to do that slowly.

ANGELA. Okay.

The doorbell rings.

Good.

RACHEL. Don't make a big deal out of it, okay?

ANGELA. No, I won't, I'm just pleased...

RACHEL. Good. I'm pleased too.

The doorbell rings again. ANGELA *flinches.*

ANGELA. Shall I get that?

RACHEL. Yes.

ANGELA. I am pleased, love, okay?

RACHEL. I'm pleased too.

ANGELA. Okay.

ANGELA exits. Nothing.

More nothing.

RACHEL shifts her shoulder, and tries to make it touch the other side of the bed. We can hear someone walking slowly up the stairs.

They take ages. RACHEL *starts to try and pull herself up the bed. She gets her muscles in a tangle, she gets caught with her right arm acting as pivot at a funny angle.*

JAMES enters the room.

JAMES. Your mum let me up...

RACHEL. Okay.

JAMES. Yeah. She seemed really pleased to see me actually. I mean...

RACHEL. Can you just – I need a hand – will you –

>JAMES *leans over and supports her back*. RACHEL *readjusts her arm. She's comfortable.*

JAMES (*with one of his smiles*). Hi.

>*Blackout.*

ACT FOUR

4.1

6th March.

She's asleep. PETER *stands about five metres from her bed. He makes as if to move, to sit down. But changes his mind and just remains standing proud.*

He doesn't say anything.

Pause.

PETER. Rach?

He sits down, and then stands up again, and moves backwards from the bed.

Pause. He notices the wheelchair and walks over and touches it. He then turns away from it as if spotted. He is prowling.

He takes off his jumper, he struggles with it slightly.

Rachel... Rach?

RACHEL (*growling with post-sleep*). Con...

PETER. Hi.

Pause. She registers him, she pulls back.

Hi. I, uh, I'm –

Pause. She tries to shift away from him. She's still slightly asleep.

Hi. Rachel?

Pause.

I just really wanted... to talk to you. Your mum's making dinner, so I thought... you'd need to be awake in a bit, if you like… Do you still want that bed bath? I thought it'd be good to wash – (*Half-laugh*.) before dinner.

Pause. He scratches himself and waits. She turns and looks at him.

Hi.

RACHEL. Okay.

Pause. RACHEL *tries to sit up, he moves as if to help her, but she knows what she's doing now. She puts a pillow from her head underneath her back. Then she pulls herself up using hands on the bedboard, the pillow getting lower and lower down her back as she does. Finally she's in semi-sitting position.* PETER *watches this in awed silence.*

Pause. She looks at him carefully, he looks back.

PETER. Oh. I saw the maddest thing… I was walking, when I was going… home… A man was sitting in his car, listening to his radio. It wasn't that strange. But he looked pretty intense. I thought he was probably listening to the football or something, or he'd had an argument and gone outside to sit in the car. I don't know, but it felt really strange. And then I got scared he was gassing himself, and that I didn't notice, so I went back to check, and he noticed I was checking and smiled at me. It wasn't that mad, it felt pretty strange. He was probably listening to the football.

Pause.

And I've given up the football team… county, I mean… Baylis was really pissed off – 'the first school representative for years' – but it was making me feel too important.

RACHEL (*quiet*). Where have you been?

PETER. I don't know. Listen. Can I do anything? I mean, it doesn't have to be –

RACHEL. Okay. (*Beat*.) You need to buy me some tampons.

PETER. Okay.

RACHEL. I just don't want to ask Mum. She'll just fuss, she got me some last week, but I'm…

PETER. I'll get them. Is there a particular sort? Or…

RACHEL. Whatever's cheapest. Heavy flow.

PETER. Heavy flow, okay.

RACHEL. Take the money out of my top drawer?

PETER. No. I can get it.

RACHEL. Peter –

PETER. No. I've got it. Is there any particular – brand – you prefer?

RACHEL. You want to buy me tampons as a present?

PETER. No.

> RACHEL *begins to giggle,* PETER *joins in. She then stops, and looks careful again.*

I'm just pleased you want me back. To give them to you…

RACHEL. Arsched said to say like you weren't coming back – think like –

PETER. Well, he was wrong. I want to be back –

RACHEL. Why?

PETER. Because I want to be… I think that's a pretty good reason…

> *Pause.* RACHEL *shifts her bum slightly, using her hands,* PETER *notices.*

Is it urgent? Do you want me to get them now?

RACHEL. Yeah. I'm bleeding all over the bed.

> *Pause. He moves his foot and then regrets it.*

PETER. Your mum seemed pleased to see me. Though you've been talking, the two of you, yeah?

RACHEL. Did you know James came round?

PETER. Yeah?

RACHEL. He said you hadn't been in school… for a while.

PETER. No.

RACHEL. He asked whether he could do anything. I said,
'How's Alice?' and he got really defensive about that
because I'd been a bitch to her when she came round – I said
I thought you fancied her and he laughed.

PETER. No.

RACHEL. He said that he'd told you that we hadn't been
together long enough for all this – effort –

Pause.

He said he'd said to you he didn't think I was worth it – all
this trouble, all this effort and stuff you're doing. He said he
didn't want you doing it all just because you felt you had to
or because you felt sorry for me and that he had told you
that, and that it was unfair of me to expect so much of you.
Because it wasn't your fault I'm like this. You weren't doing
enough other stuff, other than me, I was basically sort of
eating you up. He said he wasn't going behind my back, he
wasn't that kind of guy, anything he said to you about me, he
wanted to say to my face as well. So he did – he came round
to see me just so he wasn't talking behind my back. Which is
quite an effort, just so you aren't talking behind someone's
back. You're his best friend so he felt he should stick up for
you, or help you, or say things to me about you – um… I
think he was quite worried about you – being missing. So,
anyway, that was all funny – considering what I know about
him and Alice. Do you think there's something wrong with
him and Alice? Because I do. Anyway, I thought it was quite
brave of him. Though I can't stand up so…

PETER (*close*). He shouldn't have said that.

RACHEL. Was that what you were thinking? Were you –

PETER. No. No. I mean, we're not that – we're not that – close
– any more –

RACHEL (*soft, quick*). Me and you?

PETER. No. No. James.

RACHEL. Is Alice the reason you argued?

PETER. No. You. Listen, what he said –

RACHEL. She likes you, I think – James is quite rough. Some of the things she said.

PETER. Yeah? But I'm here with you.

RACHEL. But I think most of the stuff is stuff she does. She basically tells him to treat her like shit. She's that kind of girl…

PETER. No. She's not.

RACHEL. Do you fancy her?

PETER. No… I fancy you.

Beat.

RACHEL (*quiet*). Do you want to give me that bed bath?

PETER. Okay.

Beat. He lets go of her leg. Neither of them look at each other.

RACHEL (*nervous, but with a brilliant face on it*). You need to go and get a – there's a basin in the bathroom with a sponge in it and some special soap, fill that up, fill it in the bath, or using the shower otherwise it'll take ages –

PETER. Okay.

He hesitates and then exits, RACHEL waits.

She doesn't try and do anything, she just waits, steely-eyed.

Pause. She scratches her nose, touches her scar, smells her hand.

Pause.

Finally, PETER re-enters, clutching the basin, careful not to spill it.

RACHEL. Put it on the floor.

PETER. Okay.

RACHEL. Have you put the soap in the water?

PETER. I wasn't sure to – before I poured it – you said it was special soap so…

RACHEL. Put some in now, it's fine.

PETER. I could do it again.

RACHEL. No. Don't.

Beat. PETER *adds soap to the water, and then swirls it round.*

Get the sponge wet.

PETER *does.*

Really squeeze it out, as much as you can.

PETER. Okay.

RACHEL. Now just sponge me down…

PETER. You don't just want to do it yourself…

Beat. She undoes her straps, ready for the top to be taken off. He watches.

RACHEL. I could do my front if you want…

PETER. Okay.

RACHEL (*forced giggle*). But that's the best bit…

PETER. No. You can do it.

RACHEL. I want you to do it.

PETER. Can I do your back first?

RACHEL. Yeah. Help me turn.

He helps her. Then he starts to wipe her back carefully with the cloth. He does so very methodically, lifting up her arms and her hair to get to the places where he thinks she needs cleaning.

Alice likes you, I think, James is quite… rough. Some of the things she said.

PETER. Yeah?

RACHEL. But I think most of it is stuff she does. She basically tells him to treat her like shit, she's that kind of girl...

PETER. I think that's... done.

RACHEL. Turn me over then.

With his help, she turns over onto her front. She makes to cover her breasts, but then changes her mind and makes them as exposed as possible.

PETER. You don't need your face...

RACHEL. No.

He carefully wipes down her body, they hardly breathe. He eventually finishes, he's being so careful, it's beautiful. He finishes and they sit in silence.

PETER. We should get you walking after this...

RACHEL. I've got a wheelchair now.

PETER. Yeah. I saw, I thought that was... great.

Beat. PETER *gingerly moves forward and puts* RACHEL*'s straps back on, he hides her breasts for her. She lets him.*

RACHEL. What did you really do? When you weren't in school.

PETER. Oh. Um. Walked about. There was a pub where I played the slots a bit. I lost a bit. But... I just walked about mostly, went into shops. But, uh...

RACHEL. Why did you put my straps back on?

PETER. I don't know.

RACHEL. Okay. Now you need to do the bottom half.

PETER. I know.

Pause. They just look at each other.

RACHEL. There's no. Blood.

PETER. Yeah, okay...

RACHEL. Help me turn over again...

PETER. Okay.

He tries to help her turn over, but doesn't want to put much effort into it.

RACHEL. Peter –

He tries again, this time, she turns easily. He lifts up her gown, she pulls her knickers down to her mid-thighs and he, thinking it's a hint, pulls them all the way off and places them beside her on the bed. She says nothing and he starts slowly to clean her. Very, very gently. Then, after he finishes that side, he wordlessly half-lifts her and pulls her back onto her front and then cleans her some more, going all the way down to her feet, he spends a lot of time on her feet. Then he finishes.

PETER. Done.

RACHEL. Okay, just, uh, go to the bathroom and pour it all away. Just leave it how you found it.

PETER. Who did you last time?

RACHEL. The nurse did me a couple of times, then my mum…

PETER. Okay.

He picks up the basin and exits. RACHEL *pulls herself down in the bed, so she's back in a lying position. She checks her body, all over, with her hand.* PETER *re-enters.*

RACHEL. Sit on the bed, would you?

PETER. I don't…

RACHEL. Lie down, with me, please…

PETER *hesitates, then gets on the bed.*

I want to be facing you…

PETER. Okay.

PETER *turns her, helps her turn, and then lies down beside her, so that the two of them are facing each other, she strokes his face.*

RACHEL. Can I tell you something –

PETER. Yeah.

RACHEL. I followed him because I was scared –

PETER. No. I didn't mean that… question. It wasn't a question.

RACHEL. But I don't want those questions with you –

PETER. I know.

RACHEL. When they first did the photofit – he looked like my dad.

PETER. Oh.

RACHEL. I couldn't get it right. (*Laugh*.) The police wanted to talk to him until they found out… he was dead.

PETER. Okay.

RACHEL. When they showed me the photofit – they said – does that remind you of anyone and I said, 'Yes,' because I realised and they said, 'Who?' And I said, 'That reminds me of my dad.' So they just said, 'Is your dad still at home with you? Billy, can you call the Social in?' And I said, 'My dad's dead,' and I saw Billy – the one they call Billy, I didn't really know him – almost laugh. Because it was quite funny. So I smiled at him, and he just tried to stop laughing, I mean, he didn't let it out. They were really disappointed. And I didn't want you there, to see that, or… anything. I was rubbish at it.

Beat.

Take off your top.

PETER. Now?

RACHEL. I like your chest.

He takes off his top, he struggles a bit. It's difficult taking off your top when you're lying down.

I followed him because I thought if I did anything else then he'd be worse and I didn't put up much of a fight the rest of the time either. And I – when I talked about that stuff, with Arshed, the police, the doctors – I didn't want you there because I was ashamed and I was bad at it. Peter, I couldn't even tell them what he looked like – so / I made him look like my dad…

PETER. I knew that. I wasn't –

RACHEL. Do you mind if I undo my straps? I want to feel me and you…

PETER. Okay.

She undoes her straps halfway.

RACHEL. I don't want to have sex.

PETER. No.

RACHEL. It's okay. I'm still not… ready.

PETER. Yeah.

RACHEL. Okay.

Pause, she undoes the remainder of her straps. Then they lie there, in an odd but perfectly formed shape. They try not to breathe.

(*Soft.*) I don't think I'd be able to… feel it… anyway… sometimes I can feel it though, when I pee… so…

PETER. Yeah?

RACHEL. But I don't think I'd feel it and that would be…

PETER. Yeah.

RACHEL. When it's our first time, I want it to be about us… Not… I don't want things left to chance.

PETER. No. I'm not – ready – either…

Pause. PETER clears his throat.

RACHEL. I'm sorry you won't be… first.

PETER. No. That's okay.

RACHEL. This feels amazing.

PETER. Yeah.

RACHEL. I love you.

Beat.

Will you take your trousers off…

PETER. I'm…

RACHEL. That's okay, I'm expecting it.

PETER *does. This takes him a minute, he's not sure how to do it.*

Will you help me take everything off…

PETER. Okay.

They pull her nightie over her head, there's a brief moment of tangle, but then it's all okay.

RACHEL. This feels amazing, doesn't it?

PETER. I love you too.

RACHEL. Okay.

Beat.

PETER. Are you okay?

RACHEL. No. This is good for me. I think. This is –

PETER. Are you, uh…

RACHEL. I think I can feel you, in my legs, I think I can feel your legs.

PETER. Can you?

RACHEL. Do you want to take your boxer shorts off?

PETER. No.

RACHEL. Okay. Kiss me.

He does. She ventures a hand down his body.

PETER. No. Don't.

RACHEL. It's just a hand.

PETER. No. Don't.

They lie together forever. The Archers *theme music starts playing from downstairs,* RACHEL *giggles through her snot.*

Pause.

(*Soft.*) Are you – crying?

RACHEL. This is better. We'll stay like this – okay?

PETER. Yeah.

RACHEL. It'll be worth it soon – I'll let you – we can make love –

PETER. No. That's not important –

RACHEL. Well, now you know anyway –

PETER. No –

RACHEL. Cuddle me – now you know –

PETER. Okay.

RACHEL. Tighter –

PETER. Okay…

RACHEL. I love you.

PETER. I love you too.

Long pause. She tries to feel closer to him.

RACHEL. I want to turn over, I want you around me, is that okay? I want you tucked up into me. I don't mind. If I can feel anything… I don't mind that…

Beat.

PETER. Okay.

He effects some of this, their bodies spoon. He tries to hold his groin as far away from her as possible. That's an almost impossible task. She tries to nestle in. Then tries again. Then tries a third time. She looks confused, and then upset.

RACHEL. This feels nice.

PETER. Yeah.

She nestles in a fourth time. Moving her back down to him.

RACHEL. You're not…

PETER. No. Not yet.

RACHEL. It's gone down?

Pause. PETER *tries again to move away from her, but there's no room for that.* RACHEL*'s perma-smile fades.*

I was just expecting it...

PETER. Yeah?

RACHEL (*soft*). It wasn't something... I did?

PETER. No.

Pause. She picks up his forearm and studies it, he tries to lean over her to see what she's doing, but he can't. Again, it's difficult him being on the bed.

RACHEL (*small*). You do still fancy me?

PETER. Yeah.

She traces a few of the lines on his hand.

RACHEL. I know I don't look amazing... but... It doesn't matter. We can be friends.

PETER. No, we're – you're my girlfriend.

RACHEL (*perfectly soft*). Has anyone tried anything?

PETER. What?

RACHEL. Any of the other girls? Libby? Nicky? Ruth?

PETER. No.

RACHEL (*a delicious forced giggle*). They will. You're quite fanciable really. I should do an erection test. Say their name, describe what they look like, and I know them naked, see if you get one... Libby – let's see – at a guess, 32C – big, long nipples, she walks around naked in the girl's dressing rooms, though her arse is bigger than you'd expect. She tried to shave herself once, and cut it... Alice, short stubby nipples, no room, Libby's spread out, hers don't... this stomach which tips slightly over her knickers, not fat, muscle... this perfect arse...

They both stiffen.

Okay. That's okay.

PETER. I'm getting off the bed.

RACHEL. No! DON'T! No!

He half-falls and half-dismounts the bed.

Pause. He's trying to hold in his erection.

PETER. Sorry.

Pause. She isn't sure what to do.

RACHEL. Do you want a blow job? I think I could do one of those. Do you? You'll have to come closer.

Pause.

I don't mind, Peter. Honestly.

PETER. No.

Pause. He starts to shuffle back away from her, and then stops. They stand there for ages.

Listen – (*Soft.*) Do you really think I can help?

RACHEL. Help what?

PETER. You.

RACHEL. You're supposed to want to see me.

PETER. Yeah?

RACHEL. I think I understand why you're going better than you do.

PETER. No, I'm not... leaving...

Pause. RACHEL touches her scar.

RACHEL. You should stop being friends with James –

PETER. I know.

RACHEL. But don't... Alice – don't rescue her – because she doesn't need it – that's just the way she is – girly, she's not really worth much... She enjoys being a victim too much. Plastic.

PETER. That wasn't Alice, the erection, it wasn't you talking about Alice. It was you, I mean, lying with you, and you kept sticking your bum harder into me when you were telling me about how… I mean, you could have been talking about anyone naked, it was really nice… and just so, with your bum sticking into me. I think you're really pretty, and it was you that gave me the… I'm not put off, and no one… That's what my mum thought, but that's not what…

RACHEL. Okay. Thanks.

PETER. No. No. Don't say thanks.

Pause. RACHEL's shoulders slump, gradually and completely. Until there's almost nothing left.

RACHEL (*slow and soft*). I… I never really liked it when you were here – we always got it wrong, didn't we? I liked you visiting for the bits in between – the bits when you weren't here – when I could dream or plan your next visit – when I could – you're really good to dream about, Peter, you're that kind of person. So it didn't matter when your visits were shit because they were only two or three hours long – or one hour sometimes – and there were twenty or thirty or forty hours in between your visits and I used to just think about you – about how we'd get it right next time. You filled up my brain – and that was – great – when I was just waiting – to get better. Even when you weren't here for thirty days – you filled up my… So – thank you – I'm really grateful for that. I liked thinking about you – sometimes I thought the wrong thing but… you were the good bit. Most of the time, you were something good to think about. So don't be hard on yourself, okay? You did really well.

Beat. He moves his body as if to sit on the bed. But he doesn't move his feet.

But the thing is… I think maybe, if I'm going to get better – I'm going to have to do it without all this… effort. I just want to make everything normal. I'm not sure you can be… make me normal – I'm not sure the effort you make me… is the right kind. I am really grateful though…

Pause.

Did you ever even want to be here?

PETER (*careful, in case he gets the words wrong*). I want to be here now.

Beat.

RACHEL. Okay.

The lights slowly fade, PETER just stands there, in his boxers, unsure whether to put his clothes on again or not.

Blackout.

Music: 'If You Could See Her' from Cabaret.

The End.

STACY

For Chris Hannan

Stacy was first performed at the Arcola Theatre, London, on 6 February 2007, performed by Arthur Darvill.

Director	Hamish Pirie
Designer	Beck Rainford
Lighting Designer	David Plater
Composers	Max and Ben Ringham
Sound Designer	Helen Atkinson

The play was subsequently revived at the Trafalgar Studios, London, on 2 October 2007, performed by Ralf Little.

Stacy was originally workshopped in front of an audience at the Tron Theatre, Glasgow, where it was performed by Tommy Mullins, directed by Carrie Cracknell, produced by Hush Productions and resourced by the National Theatre of Scotland.

Characters

ROB, *26, ordinary-looking*

A SLIDE PROJECTOR

ROB *is sitting on a chair, beside him is a slide projection unit.*

Up on the projector as the audience enter is a picture of Stacy, 25 – Stacy is pretty and made-up to look like she doesn't care. She's wearing a funny smile (because she says she doesn't like having her photo taken).

ROB *holds the slide gun in his hand; sometimes he operates the machine and sometimes it's done automatically. Every time a slide changes the machine makes a loud noise.*

A man at the back gives a thumbs-up to show ROB *he can start talking.* ROB *acknowledges the hand and then starts.*

I was at Stacy's street by about 7.15...

He presses the slide gun, it shows a picture of a street.

...and the air was the sort of evening mist you sometimes get which you know is bad for you. Anyway, a car came around the corner and I actually pulled out of the headlights of it, so... I don't know why. But she lived at Number 33b.

Slide – a numbered tile – '33b'.

The road wasn't one with odds on one side and evens on the other, it went chronologically up one side and then just swapped over the road and carried on counting up over there. Which made it further to walk to Number 33.

Slide – an Olympic walker looking knackered.

ROB *turns and looks at it and laughs.*

I'd bought a bottle of wine too (and I couldn't find an off-licence so I paid pub prices for it, which shows I was desperate to make a good impression, particularly as I knew she had wine in, half of which I'd paid for), so part of me wanted to get her pissed, and... seduce her – which wasn't likely by the way – and sort it out that way.

I did have this thing I was planning to say though…

Slide – Hugh Grant.

He turns and looks again and laughs.

'I'm the sort of guy who falls in love really easily, honestly I am, I can fall in love in a night, but that's not the same as what I'm feeling now and I honestly didn't realise it till last night. I'd like to just try and behave like more than friends, just to see if it works, because things have changed now, and I know you probably don't fancy me (though she'd been wet during the sex so I obviously was okay) but…'

And then I'd just leave it hanging at the end. Like that isn't me not finishing the speech, that is the speech. A cheesy and very very pathetic speech but at least she'll have to respond to it. She won't be interested in a relationship but it's not about that, she'll have to respond to it, basically, and I don't mind being humiliated.

Basically, she could still respond with 'Let's not talk about it now'; that's a worst case scenario. Because I can't say 'I want to talk about it now' without sounding like a dick. Then when I bought it up at some future appropriate date with 'Are you ready to talk about it now?', she'd probably respond with, 'Let's leave it, the past is the past'– she loves phrases like that. Ones you can write on your forehead, do you know what I mean? But that's the worst case scenario.

I stop at gate 17,

Slide – a numbered tile '17'.

because I want to think about my speech, but eventually I get to 33b

Slide – a numbered tile '33b'.

and I stop there as well. She wouldn't be home yet anyway, because she doesn't get home till eight most of the time on weeknights (I'm home at 5.30 – another advantage of my job, and I don't leave the house till 8.30 whereas she's out by eight at the latest). But it probably wouldn't be a great idea to wait outside the house for her to come home, so I ring the bell and hope the landlord or Shona's in,

Slide – Shona's face. She's slightly overweight and she isn't ugly but she isn't confident either so the good bits of her face tend to be pretty well hidden.

as I have no idea what she does and I certainly have no idea what the landlord does so it could be either of them are in. I don't even have an idea why Shona

Slide – Shona.

and Stacy

Slide – Stacy.

are living together, but I think, THINK, this might be Shona's rental.

Slide – Shona.

I think she signed the lease from Mr Martin and Stacy's

Slide – Stacy.

living in it via Shona,

Slide – Shona.

and just took it through *Time Out* or whatever. I bet she's paying 'mate's rates' though – the thing about Stacy

Slide – Stacy.

is she's a brilliant negotiator. Even if Shona

Slide – Shona.

didn't know her before. So I ring on the door but Shona doesn't answer so I just wait in the cold, on their tiny tiny porch, and I have to take my coat off to sit on because I'm not sitting on the ground, not with an arse like mine.

Slide – Charlie Chaplin – in The Kid *– sitting on a kerb-edge.*

They're 33b but actually there's no separate entrance for A or B, in fact there is no A, it's 33 and 33b. B is just the second floor and you have to walk through A's front room to get to the staircase to get up there. Apparently it's illegal for them to be sold like that but it's only renting; the people in A, or the one person in A – Mr Martin – owns B as well. I sit on the step in front of the door, and sort of on top of my coat, it's not exactly comfy but my arse is warm.

I started getting piles aged fourteen and I didn't tell anyone for ages, and tried to deal with it myself, I even went to a chemist to buy some pile cream and the chemist believed it was for my gran. I read books on it secretly, books I took from the library, and I was even embarrassed for taking it then – which is the advantage of the internet now, for kids like that. Anyway I worked out it was sort of a piece that had popped out of my bum and to get it wet and then push it back in. I tried that in a hot bath, it worked, then the pile kept popping up again so I was constantly pushing it back in. Then my pile, when I was trying to shit, exploded, and you have never seen so much blood. I started howling, my mum

Slide – Mum. Unsmiling but pretty. She's fiftyish and she dies her hair dark brown.

came in and tried to calm me down but she was more upset than she needed to be and she rushed me to casualty.

We got done by this really really junior doctor, and I think it would have been much worse for an older person (and Stacy's

Slide – Stacy.

adventures in KY jelly with another doctor were far worse), and he put a lot of padding on it and told me to make an appointment with outpatients (and we did, but this is what my mum's

Slide – Mum.

like: she broke the appointment, cancelled it, when she discovered I wasn't bleeding any more, which I briefly wasn't, but, actually I'm still bleeding till today, so… but she said she didn't want to put me through getting the pile sewn up – they put a band around it – and that if it continued I could get it sorted out when I was older), and told me to eat more fibre, fruit and drink more water. But I already did loads of that, I think it was a reaction to my sister, or I do when I'm feeling dramatic… Like when I'm trying to do a speech like that…

I met a girl at a party and we were hardly talking at all but we got talking – it turns out she started her period really early; aged eight – and she sort of knew but sort of also thought she was bleeding to death (very very heavy flow – always has been – she said it disables her two days of the month, she can hardly move and she has to take them as holiday because her boss – a woman – says that regular illness is the invalid's own responsibility – so she doesn't get holiday – (*Laughs*.) the really weird thing about it was she was trying to chat me up I think). Anyway, it really shows up on the enamel of the toilet bowl – now, when it happens – I sit on a toilet seat and let it bleed because I can't think of anything else to do.

Debbie

Slide – Debbie.

said actually not to… no, I'm not going to tell you that yet… No. Sorry.

Debbie's

Blank slide.

from work. Another confusion actually…

Anyway, I phone my brother again,

Slide – brother. A lot better-looking than ROB, *and he knows it.*

and I never phone my brother, and he's not in so I leave a message asking him to phone me. Then I phone my mum,

Slide – Mum.

and I get through. 'Hello?' – she always sounds as if she's surprised that telephones actually work – I disconnect the call, I breathed into it for a few seconds but I didn't have anything to say and she didn't repeat 'Hello?' again, and she doesn't know how to use 1471.

Anyway.

He turns to look at his mum, he stands up and walks slightly forward to the audience.

It started, with Stacy,

He indicates his mum's picture, he doesn't change the slide.

because she was upset, she'd asked for a hug, then she'd kissed me, I'd got an erection, she'd noticed – in fact she'd laughed and told me she noticed – and then it got passionate quite quickly.

I always actually worry I'm going to smell or something else – like one of the things girls seem to do more of now, is to put their hands inside your arse – now (a) I've had a lot of bleeding trouble with my arse

Slide – arse.

– as has Stacy –

Slide – Stacy.

(b) I can never get it properly clean – it's always sweaty and sticky, I don't know how other people do it; (c) there doesn't seem much point – Stacy even tried it (despite her arse problems) but I moved her hand away – twice – that made me feel like a girl actually, which was quite funny.

She hadn't shaved herself – I actually think that's more of a working-class thing (a throwback from the age of pubic lice?) – and I sort of tried to get that right but I wasn't very good at it. I was out of practice, and she was tugging at me too but girls are never in practice at that. Then suddenly she was sort of guiding me towards her and pushing me in, whilst underneath me. The (two) girls that have been in charge of me in the past had always been on top before, and I always felt blow jobs came first, so this was surprising. Then we finished and I was on top and asked whether I should roll off now because they'd always got off first before – and she said yes and I'd sort of rolled off and then turned on my side to look at her, because she looked incredible.

But she kept her eyes shut and her tits (the only disappointing thing about her, they felt too fleshy rather than firm, and felt fat if you know what I mean, and I'm not a big fan of big tits anyway) were kind of sagging over and she moved her hand down her body and began masturbating herself, working herself up. And I, obviously, had no idea what to do (I struggle with fucking bras after all). After a while I tried to join in but she had too good a rhythm going and her hand was obviously underneath and I never know the exact right place to go neither. So I sort of just put my hand on top of hers and went up and down with her hands, I did none of the work but attempted to feel part of the work. Then I put my face really close to hers so I could feel her breathing, I actually like the smell of bad breath after sex. But she didn't respond to that neither, so I just left her and she orgasmed eventually. On her own. Then she'd rolled over away from me.

Anyway, that wasn't supposed to happen. We've actually been friends since we were kids, and that was last night. So...

No. I mean it's not like...

I spotted Shona

Slide – Shona.

quite late, she was struggling with some shopping and it was cold and she was losing circulation on those blue plastic carrier bags that are cheaper than the supermarket ones that cut into your fingers. So I would have helped, but I only heard her when she was about five doors away.

Shona smiles and looks nervous when she sees me, I do the odd gawky thing my dad

Slide – blank, no face at all.

ROB *turns to look at it and laughs.*

sometimes does of saying 'Hi' with my shoulders. She smiles again. 'Hi' she says, and I don't reply to that either, I just breathe out through my nose in quite a satisfying way and raise my eyebrows. So we stand opposite each other about six feet apart and she tries to keep smiling.

'Nice day?'

'Yeah,' she says, and she hands me the other bags quite confidently (so I'm not carrying all of them), fiddles her key out of her pocket and undoes the door. 'Come in,' she says. 'Aren't you cold?'

We walk through Mr Martin's front room, which is one of those scary front rooms that's meant for 'presentation' only, and the sofa has covers put on them the rest of the time. Beige plastic covers so as to fit with the room (imagine colour-coding your sofa covers), and then the rest of it looks so fucking cold: several crap pictures of birds and a stuffed falcon on a perch on top of an upright piano, two sofas covered in beige covers slightly lighter than the colour of the walls. The stairs going up to B were pine and nice but had a beige central carpet, and just went straight up, there was no curve at either end, this was a modern house (and I like a house with an ambitious staircase).

B was all light yellow, I remember how pleased Stacy

Slide – Stacy.

was when it got done and how pissed off that I didn't notice immediately on entering the house (especially as I'd been told already about the paint job and enthused about it in the context of something else). That had been the issue for a while.

'Do you want some tea?' Shona

Slide – Shona.

asks, before we've hardly got up the stairs, she doesn't really know why I'm here.

'Yeah. Thanks. I'm just waiting for Stacy,

Slide – Stacy.

if that's okay?'

'Yeah. Okay.' Shona

Slide – Shona.

was one of those people who are a bit too nice. Like this morning, when Stacy

Slide – Stacy.

had kicked me out of bed, Shona

Slide – Shona.

woke me – 'Sorry, I didn't know if you wanted waking, Rob.

Slide – of our ROB. *Like Stacy,* ROB *also attempts to convince any photographer that he hates having his photo taken.*

But I figured... if you... Are you working?' And then she tried to get me breakfast and she wasn't wearing a bra when I was talking to her because she was still in her nightie and she has this weird thing where she tenses her left breast. Not that I can see it now because she's still in her coat and work things.

I walk through the house into Stacy's room.

Slide – Stacy.

I leave Shona

Slide – Shona.

to take the chance to busy herself in the kitchen, and it's a phrase which suits her.

Stacy's room

Slide – Stacy. Then a series of shots which show her room. It's much as he describes it. The wardrobe door is focused upon in these shots.

is pretty bland, she has a bland DVD collection, a bland CD collection. Her clothes are more her, she can be adventurous at times, she doesn't wash them regularly enough but at this moment I don't mind that, I even climb inside the wardrobe, partly because I made a pact with myself not to do anything to upset her intimacy, and I don't think standing in a wardrobe would upset her but it feels intimate to me. I don't stay in there long.

Shona

Slide – Shona.

enters carrying both teas, and she got changed out of her work things into a light-blue top with slight straps (a summer top in November, the first clue of the night).

Slide – the powder-blue top, it's pretty low-cut, some nipples sticking out of it.

ROB *turns round a moment to look at it, then turns back to us with a grin.*

Debbie said…

Slide – Debbie, and then the slides reverse back to the powder-blue top.

and some light-blue jeans.

'Are you okay?' she asks.

'Yeah.' She puts down the tea on Stacy's

Slide – Stacy.

chest of drawers and smiles back, then she sits on the bed.

And so I sit beside her.

'So are you two… together now, then?' She asks. No, we just had sex.

Slide – hardcore porn shot, the moment of penetration.

And, honestly, the funny thing about having sex

Slide – another hardcore porn shot.

with your best friend is that they are a lot better at sex

Slide – another hardcore porn shot.

than you thought she would be and you're a lot worse.

'I don't know.'

'I thought you were just friends.' She said.

'Yeah, well, we could just be.'

'What does she say?'

'I think she just wants to be friends. Or I know that… I'm not even supposed to be here now really.' I laugh, and sort of stand there and Shona

Slide – Shona.

smiles bravely back. They're not really friends, the landlord made it a condition of the lease that neither of the tenants upstairs were friends, Shona's tried a few times (bought Stacy

Slide – Stacy.

gifts, that sort of thing) but Stacy's not that interested, we even talked about it. She thinks Shona's

Slide – Shona.

a bit pathetic, but I quite like her. Though I'm starting to feel really tired, because I was on their sofa all night, and they don't have the heating system on properly in their house and I'm fucking cold.

When I was a kid, and that wasn't that long ago, there was this thing with this dog. He got knocked down by someone in the street and we seemed to live… we actually lived in a cul-de-sac. We were the young family in a street of retirement homes and they fucking loved us for that of course. Then this dog got knocked down in the cul-de-sac, none of our dogs, a stray, I think, but I don't know whether those really exist, it was an unknown dog, like a… But it wasn't dead, it was whining and thrashing and no one wanted to do anything about it. Apart from my sister, who was always pretty loud, one of these people who made quite a lot of noise. I made quite a lot of noise too, but I was better at it than her. She went out and looked at it, and stood there ages staring and then Mr Parker, who's about eighty, came out and tried to get her away. And then a whole convention of these retired people came out and all stood around Mr Parker trying to get this screaming wriggly girl out of the way, because she didn't fucking care that they were old and didn't really respect the fact that they would break more easily. And so my parents had to come out and the dog was still whining and thrashing. My dad was one of these people that was pretty unspectacular, but still thought he was right about everything. Like, 'Why are we living in a cul-de-sac, Dad?' 'Well, son, because it's a great place to grow up, it's like having fifty grannies,' but it wasn't, it was like living in a place where you didn't bring your friends back because if you did Mr Parker would come over and start talking about the thing you were last talking about with him. Which was cricket or something embarrassing. Though he was great to talk to most of the time…

They all loved me, the pensioners, that was a good thing. I'm good with old people, I'm the sort of person who'd probably have fitted in better in the 1940s. I still am. But as a kid it was more like that, I was also beautiful, which was quite important, because old people are letches around beautiful children... And my parents loved it, and my sister hated it, she was crap with the old people and my brother just let it ride. Like he let a lot of it ride. My brother was pretty quiet about most of that stuff. But I wasn't going to bring my friends around, because I had them too, and I was quite sensible and knew it wouldn't be good.

Probably I was just better with them because the old people sort of swarmed around me because I was a pretty child, I was a beautiful child. My sister and my brother never were, and I don't know why.

Anyway, my dad made this big deal about saying that he'd deal with the dog. And told everyone they had to get off the road because he was going to have to kill it, and one of the old ladies said, 'No, let's call the RSPCA,' and Mr Parker said he didn't think this was a case for the RSPCA and we had to stand there while they discussed it whether it was a case for the fucking RSPCA and when they finished my dad, who never interrupted anyone, said, 'No, I'll deal with it.' And we all went back inside, but everyone was watching from their respective windows and everyone was trying to work out what they'd do. My dad went and got a brick and then stood there for ages and then he kneeled down beside the dog, and then he got up again and went and got an old tea towel and put that over the dog's head and then kneeled down again and then hit it really hard with the brick. Quite a few times, until it was quiet. And then he came inside and went to the bathroom and threw up and he left the dog out there with the tea towel over its head. So he didn't pull it away. He was quite odd like that, my dad, he had a strange idea what dealing with it meant.

It's funny now.

Anyway, the really funny thing was, the dog wasn't dead, it was just knocked out or something and my dad hadn't done it properly. But no one was going to say anything, my sister tried, but Mum smacked her and said she'd caused enough trouble

and she kept quiet. But the dog started howling. Literally
'howwwwwwwwwwwl' – do you know what I mean? It had a
broken jaw or something, like my dad had hit it a few times,
and had probably broken quite a few things in its head, but he
hadn't killed it, and the dog wasn't howling normally, because
he had a fucked skull and a fucked jaw and everything, but he
was making quite a lot of noise. And we all just left it, even all
the old people, because we were frightened of upsetting my
dad. Mr Parker was always saying I should respect my dad
more and that's what he was doing, respecting him. And my dad
didn't go out again because he was frightened and someone else
would do it. Anyway, by the next morning the dog had been
moved and there wasn't even a stain on the street. I think it was
probably Mr Parker, during the night. That's how you behave
with dignity, I think.

I know why I thought about that too.

My brother was away actually, on Scout camp but I don't know
that would have changed anything.

*He turns around to look at the slide projection screen,
smiles, and then starts to walk away from it. Then he turns
back and looks at us with a smile. He brushes down his lap,
even though he's had nothing on it.*

'Did you...' Shona swallows, then she stops saying anything,
torn between her need to keep friends with Stacy

Slide – Stacy.

(which would mean kicking me out) and her need to have me in
the house because, and this I know for a fact, she fancies me.
Anyway, she just dances around and says, 'Did you...'

'Listen, don't worry about it. It's a lot of stuff.' Her left breast
tenses again, she sees me look at it and blushes. 'She won't
mind too much.'

'But you two... last night.'

'Yeah, but we were both drunk, we just need to talk about it.'

'But she doesn't want to talk about it?'

'No. Not really. But I'll talk to her anyway.'

Now, we have talked already, and it was only about six hours ago but as we didn't address it and I have a strategy to get it out of her. Plus, she wouldn't have even had the closure she did have if it wasn't for the fact that I'd turned up at her office, and turning up at her house was actually a better place. What she actually said was – 'You're my best friend, Rob,

   Slide – Rob.

my absolute best, I don't have anyone like you, I feel better when you're near me, you're genuinely the most important person in my life' – Stacy is one of these people who's very uncomfortable with sincerity, so overdoes it, because she doesn't actually know what it means. Anyway, we are best friends, we've been friends since we were kids, when my mum

   Slide – Mum.

was being shit – and she wasn't that shit, I mean just a bit thoughtless or whatever, I would go to Stacy's.

   Slide – Stacy.

She came to mine as often probably. 'You're my best friend too.' I said. I'm not in love with her – I do love her, and there is a difference, though there is also a degree in which she broke my heart. And she thought she'd done it like that, by reminding me I was her best friend and not saying anything else. 'I just ordered your food,' she said, she smiled broadly and craply, placing a ticket with the number basically rubbed off on the table, her thumb was more sweaty than she thought, 'I paid for it, already,' she said, steady as a rock. 'I didn't think you'd want me to stay.' She looked like Mrs Benevolence. 'I want you to stay,' I said, with some delight, as she left me that one open. But she left anyway.

'So do you want it to happen?' Shona says.

   Slide – Shona.

Now,

   He turns to look at the slide of Shona.

she was really sweet this morning.

I don't know why but the moment felt right to kiss her. So I did, and I never kiss anyone, but I was tired and cold and she'd got dressed up for me, she'd blatantly, blatantly got dressed up for me in her best pale-blue thing and I know and have always known because Stacy

Slide – Stacy.

thought it was really funny that she fancies me. Plus she was sitting beside me on a bed which I'd had sex on less than 24 hours ago, and the sheets blatantly won't have been changed because Stacy left the house before me, and she's a dirty cow. And one thing to be said for sex after a little bit of time is that it doesn't satiate your appetite, it actually reminds you that you have one. She kissed me back, we seemed to kiss for ages, and it was genuinely nice, then she broke off and said, 'But you love Stacy.' With her big shiny soulful eyes. I laugh and kiss her again and she kissed me back. Satisfied I think.

Stacy always used to take me to these parties too, and say things about me I didn't get...

Anyway. It wasn't one of those situations where you move quickly. I sort of stroked the outside of her clothes. Shona

Slide – Shona.

was very very feely to the touch too, like her body had been made like that. She wasn't wearing a bra either, and I normally like to touch a bra but if you don't take the T-shirt

Slide – the strappy powder-blue top.

off too soon there's something brilliant and touching a naked soft breast through a T-shirt (I suppose it's an equivalent of masturbating through knickers, also a sort of fetish of mine) and feeling the nipple harden, some girls would have taken the T-shirt off themselves but Shona

Slide – Shona.

wasn't like that, she still wasn't touching me at all. Then she moved her hand up, and I actually was almost still and breathless while she did this, because it is quite sexy, the first time anyone touches you, and she sort of sensed that and almost drew a curve round the top of her head with her hand, still not touching me but watching her hand. Then we stopped kissing and she sort of gently brought the hand down on the side of my head and onto my ear, and she sort of rested in just below my ear, and round onto my neck, and moved towards me to carry on kissing me, with her hand around my neck.

So...

I moved my hands down onto her waist and felt the roughness of the jeans, I felt round the jeans onto the thigh, we're sitting on the bed so I couldn't get near the bum but I moved around to feel between her legs but as I was moving my hand towards the between she pulled my hand away with her free hand. So I sort of played thumbs with her hand and then dislocated and moved my hand around her waist again, a waist that did bag slightly over the edge of her jeans but only in a sexy way, and there was that gorgeous gap at the back of the jeans too which girls get when they sit up because they wear their jeans higher than we do, which allowed me to reach down and touch the edge of the back of her knickers and the downy hair that always comes just above that. This was perfect, I felt the sickness of this being very very perfect.

Well, a lot better anyway...

I helped her off with her top and she sat there looking soulful so I stopped everything just to look at her and she blushed as I did, but she liked it. Her breasts (and they were breasts rather than tits) were perfect, little pert sacks with puffy nipples that spread over most of them. Most girls lie back for the porn shots because they think breasts look better like that, and they do look aesthetically more beautiful like that, but they look incredible hanging from the front of a body, and Shona didn't have great posture and they sort of hung perfectly, particularly with the nipple spreading over and discolouring them. She helped me off with my top and kissed my shoulder and then my nipple, sort of clumsily, but I liked her being clumsy.

We moved faster now. We sort of pushed back on to the bed, she kept trying to kiss me whenever she could but I started to kiss down her body and then come up again, and I played with her nipple and I even bit it lightly and then I worked down to her baggy belly and then started undoing her flies, while I was down there, looking as I pulled down her jeans to mid-thighs and her knickers just lay there, half rolled down on one side, so I could see the slight beginnings of hair, puffed up in the middle. She was still wearing her shoes and they were slip-ons but she didn't kick them off but neither did she really stop me. I went back up to her face and she was grateful and kept kissing me and I started working my hand up and down her body, and I was fucking good at it, and I was getting lower and lower each time, and I'm sure to look at it my hands looked like windscreen wipers but for once it didn't matter. Then I touched the edge of her knickers, where they'd gathered, and she gasped slightly and I don't make many girls gasp and I stopped to look at her but she didn't say anything (she was looking scared but she didn't say anything, and it was from here that I started to realise she hadn't done this before) and the next time I put my hand down I went over the top of the knickers to just where I could feel the hair starting and again and again till I was down between her legs, and she wasn't resisting me and she let me touch her, and I took her hand down there too and she started masturbating with me, and it was shared masturbation, and she'd definitely done that before and together we took off the knickers. I still had my jeans on though, she was now completely naked and I still had my jeans on.

So I stopped her hand mid-flow and brought it across to touch me through the jeans and she sort of tried to masturbate me through denim (not easy, you get a handful more of denim than dick), and we'd stopped kissing by now, and I smiled at her and then undid my jeans and pulled them down and pulled my boxers down too (the same boxers from the night before) and she sort of took my dick and tried to masturbate me, but she hadn't done it before, and she looked scared and I sort of leaned in my body towards her, spread her legs slightly, and started rubbing myself against the inside of her thigh. She started to protest, and I stopped her, 'I'm not going to do anything, this isn't sex, I'm just rubbing myself, okay? Okay?' And I kissed her, I'd literally never felt this in control and we were just looking at each other and I touched her face and she was crying slightly, so I wiped some tears away with the back of my hand, gently, and I moved my hand down her body over her breasts, and down towards my dick which I took in my hand, masturbated slightly, and then put inside her, or forced inside her because she'd never done this before, the hymen was broken (or at least I think it was) but the vagina (or whatever the right fucking word is) wasn't stretched. So it took some pushing. And she made a sort of screech, so I kissed her and carried on kissing her, biting her lips, she was trying to get away from my mouth but she was beneath me on the bed and I sort of pushed her head into the bed with my mouth. I was sort of biting into her mouth in order to keep her quiet, I was almost biting her tongue but it was more her teeth, and that hurt me too. Her hands went everywhere and I grabbed one of them and held it down but the other went everywhere and just... went everywhere. She didn't speak throughout the whole thing. I think she would have though, if I'd stopped kissing her.

I think a lot of me is actually down to the fact that I was an incredibly beautiful child. Which I'm not being arrogant about and beautiful sounds like a really funny word, especially coming from me, because I don't sound like the sort of person who says stuff like that. Do I? Anyway, I was the child people would stop in the street to say, 'You are beautiful.' I was actually that child that babysitters would hold on their lap the whole night – boy and girl babysitters. Like, mostly with other children, babysitters watch TV or invite girlfriends over, with me they'd hold me so long we'd be really clammy when my parents got back. Whenever relatives were round, of the three of us – my sister, me and my brother – I was the one who'd get the attention, I'd even get better presents. But the trouble with being beautiful and finding it all a bit effortless is that you get older and it's not so effortless any more.

No. I mean...

I actually got in a fight at school, with a guy called Tom – someone – I remember him because he had a weird bulge on his forehead. Seriously, anyway, we fought because he said he was better-looking than me – we were about eight – it was quite important – now I dress like Mr Parker and I'm young but then... I was like...well, it was important.

I don't know.

She was…

When we – when we sort of – finished, and it seemed over pretty quickly, so…

She wouldn't stop crying actually. Her lip was bleeding and she was bleeding down there obviously which might mean… And she wouldn't stop crying. Not loud tears, just tears. Stacy's

Slide – Stacy.

The slide projector seems to make more noise than it has done previously. Even ROB is surprised by it.

duvet cover was a mess but I'd already thought I might clean that. I felt practical, genuinely practical. I cleaned Shona

Slide – Shona.

up using bog roll from the bathroom, I made her sit up, I kissed her on the cheek (she didn't recoil), I led her through into the bathroom, completely naked but she wasn't awake, and noticed her arse for the first time (cellulite) and I gave her a drink of water (emptying out my teacup and using that) and then I put her under the shower. She threw up over herself in the shower so I just left her in there and it was one of those bathrooms with a key in the lock on the inside, so I took that out and brought it round the outside. Then I stripped Stacy's bed,

Slide – Stacy.

and it was getting close to the time when Stacy would be home and I was actually thinking she'd be home early tonight because she was tired, but she wasn't home yet, and I put the bedclothes, Shona's

Slide – Shona.

clothes in the washer –

Slide – Ecover laundry liquid.

mine were fine-ish and I'd do them at home. I actually thought that Shona might explain her clothes and the bedclothes in the washer but might not explain mine. Stacy's

Slide – Stacy.

clothes from last night were still in the dryer so I took them out because I thought that's something Shona

Slide – Shona.

might do.

I went back up to the bathroom and opened it up and she was still in the shower. I went in there quickly with her and washed her thoroughly down below (I remember that) took her out and wrapped her in a towel and sat her on the seat they had in there. Then I went back in the shower, and emptied it of the sick, carrying the sick to the toilet, retching as I did, but the sick had mingled with the blood so I thought that might be bad.

Then I poured Shona another glass of water and crouched down opposite her, my T-shirt was soaking. I felt like a teacher.

'Sorry,' I say. She doesn't say anything, but she's stopped crying, the towel slumps forward to reveal her breasts again. 'I'm really sorry. Um, it's just the Stacy thing, it's made me quite unhappy.' I pull her towel up.

He mimics crouching down as a teacher and then pulling her towel up and then laughs.

Then I get up, wrap myself up (though I leave my wet T-shirt on – because I don't want to take it off in front of her and it seems odd taking it off in another room – and it's fucking cold outside and so it soon feels like ice, the T-shirt, so that's a sacrifice) and check Stacy's

Slide – Stacy.

room for anything and then I leave the house to go back to Croydon. I keep thinking I'll see Stacy on the street, as I walk down her road, and I almost turn off once when I see someone coming towards me, but it isn't her. I keep thinking I'll see her on the tube too, and the T-shirt does start to feel like ice, and maybe it's before, and maybe it's fear but I start shivering. And I'm almost quite pleased I do.

When my sister died – it feels like such a big WHEN, doesn't it? Something Mr Parker would say WHEN the war was on…

I was still beautiful then. And I was still the one all the relatives wanted to see, my sister took a while to die, but they came over, to see her on her deathbed, I mean, that dramatic… and even then I got the better presents. I'm not joking, though buying a nice present for someone about to die wouldn't be that great. 'You can play with it when you're better.' 'I'm dying.' 'Well, I better give it to your brother then, he's a beautiful boy…' Do you know what I mean?

The thing was, my sister wasn't one of those kids who came into a room and lit it up. She wasn't, because I was, and she was one and a half years younger. I had a little Peter Pan act I did with all my parents' friends, 'You gave me a kiss so I shall give you a button' and my sister would go over to my mum and be stroked while I was performing, but my mum was looking at me while she was stroking. She wasn't completely over-shadowed and I wasn't completely the superstar but there was that sort of dynamic. She was a beautiful child too, she just dealt with it less well than I did, I loved the attention and knew how to deal with it and she hated the fact that I had the attention. When she died I sang at her funeral, and she'd have fucking hated that, I sang 'Empty Chairs, Empty Tables' as a boy soprano, I was quite a late ball-dropper, so still soprano, and still pretty, though that was one of the last times.

Not a dry eye in the house anyway, people still reminded me about that song five years later, still do now, last time was at a dinner party at home over the summer, when we were having another deep conversation about my sister with some strangers. My mum and dad chose the tune (which in retrospect was a fucking funny choice) but I asked to have a tune to sing, so they had to find something and they weren't very cultured, or not as other people might judge it. My brother didn't do anything, the whole service, but he was five years older. He looked after us both sometimes but mostly looked after himself. Mostly we played together and he'd have to babysit every now and again. Though I would say she was closer to him than me.

They rewrote the words actually, and they made me do it over and over and the quite sick thing was, I always thought, for about two or three years afterwards they'd make me do it to relatives or something – I mean I wasn't quite the main attraction at one of their dinner parties but it was sort of 'and now Rob's going to do his song about his dead sister' when relatives (generally old) came over, and they never knew where to look, and it wasn't like they were making me relive it or anything, because they weren't, and I fucking loved performing it and didn't associate it at all (I was young and I had a big ego) but I think it was quite sick now. Anyway,

> ROB *sings his own version of 'Empty Chairs at Empty Tables' from* Les Misérables.

The thing is I'm sure you'll think that it's unbelievable but (a) my parents are quite cheap culturally and didn't realise, genuinely didn't realise and (b) people think they can get away with a lot more with song lyrics, if you listen to them they're all shit – my personal favourite is from the really really lovely bit in *Dirty Dancing* (I'm a whore for cheap romances) and the song goes 'She's like the Wind. Through my TREE.' Do you know what I mean? Patrick Swayze

> *Slide – Patrick Swayze.*

singing a song about having an erection at a beautiful lovey-dovey moment but no one notices because they're watching him drive away in his Chevy and saying will he come back, will he come back, and he does with 'No one puts Baby in the corner.' Nice. Finally (c) I'm probably camping it up way way way too much, to make it unbelievable, but it did happen.

I can't remember much about her now, I used to give her good presents – I remember that because my parents used to give me money to buy them, sometimes giving me more than they gave my brother, with the adage, 'Well, he loves giving presents, doesn't he?' The truth was they thought people loved getting presents from me. My sister knew it every time and every time when it got to her birthday and I gave her her present she'd go over and thank my mum and dad for whatever it was and then come up afterwards and thank me. She was very very clever. That was from the age of about six upwards. I even ruined nursery for her because I used to go from my school to her nursery and stay there after school, because it had a sort of play facility, and what you may not remember of nursery is no one cared what the other kids thought of you, everyone wanted to be loved by the playleaders or teachers or whoever they were, and they loved me.

I used to try and explain this to people, about why I felt guilty about it all, but they'd all think it was me showing off, I could tell that. I never told Stacy about it, I don't think I did anyway. But that's why it's difficult to explain guilty feelings, survivor guilt is bollocks, it's about knowing what you did and why you did it and how you affected that person, and it's not something my brother will ever understand.

No.

I was at East Croydon station by about nine and took the tram up the road. My brother

Slide – brother.

was watching *Spooks* as I came in. And I sat down and watched it too. I thought then I should have taken my clothes off first but I didn't. I was still cold too. It was a repeat on Bravo or Living or one of those things, the one where Lisa Faulkner got her head boiled off in chip fat.

Slide – Lisa Faulkner.

Anyway, the first thing my brother

Slide – brother.

says when I come in (and neither of us say 'hi' when we come in – we never have), 'I had two missed calls from you.'

'Yeah.'

'My phone's off when I'm working, didn't you think that?'

'Yeah. Sorry.'

'No. Just there's no point ringing. I've got a pizza in the cooker, do you want half?'

Slide – pizza. Then another slide, half a pizza.

'Yeah. Okay.' I don't know why I wanted to phone him.

Our house is small and scruffy.

Slide – series of shots of the inside of the house, it's much as ROB *describes it.*

We have a porch and most of the time we leave most of our mail in there, or all the junk and most of the envelopes (we've both developed a habit of going to the door in the morning, ripping open anything addressed to us and then leaving the envelopes on the floor; a man from Argos delivering us a new TV told me that he would have thought we'd moved out or were on holiday if I hadn't answered the door quickly). The hallway my dad

Slide – blank.

ROB *turns around again to have another look, and laughs.*

painted yellow and purple, which was pretty outrageous for him. I once worried I was going to turn into my dad, this repressed lump of turd who had nightmares about dead dogs, but I'm not. My room is the first into the house and I look out onto the street, and I sleep on the side furthest from the door (I think everyone does, I haven't met anyone who sleeps closest the door and I've slept with a few people), but that's closest to the street, so when people walk past my house when I'm asleep I could literally reach out and touch them if there wasn't a wall there. Anyway, it's yellow, and busy with posters, it looks like a student thing still.

I found things a lot easier when I was younger, I think. It wasn't that I... I didn't get worse-looking or anything like that, I just found things easier. I was a pretty child and popular and everyone told me I was great a lot, so that was good. And it wasn't my sister dying. I didn't mind that so much, well, I minded, but not so it would change my life. I just suited being younger, I was good at it. My brother was crap at being younger, my sister was fucking terrible at it, couldn't get the whine out of her voice. She might have been a good adult. But it was partly that, that made me beautiful, that I was good in comparison and then you get older and you meet people like Stacy and she just is in a different league really.

No. About ten years ago or something I think I could have given Stacy a run for her money. Now? No.

Then there's a staircase (which leads to my brother's room, which is directly above mine, a bathroom and a guest bedroom (we have a guest bedroom, I sleep in it every now and again when my brother's really noisy). Then the living room, which you have to walk through to get to the kitchen. The living room is full of my stuff too, I collect videos and DVDs and I have seven shelves of them. It's yellow too, and has a sofa, which my brother sits on, and an easy chair, which is now really really greasy (the sofa isn't for some reason but you really notice it on the chair), we eat dinner off our laps but there's also a table at the back of the room, and a large phone. The prevailing theme in our house is yellow, like the prevailing scheme (and Stacy's

Slide – Stacy.

house is schemed not themed) of Stacy's, she came round and then copied it, though my dad

Slide – finally we see his dad's face. He looks great, he's a man who's suited his face better the older he's got.

chose the colours, and ours is strong yellow whereas hers is wishy-washy – everyone's got wishy-washy yellow though so although she said she copied it (and I was oddly oddly chuffed about it) she didn't, hers looks like loads of houses, ours looks vivid and dangerous.

'You look tired,' my brother says.

Slide – brother.

'I'm just hungry,' I say.

'Do you want anything with it?' he says. 'It's too late to put chips on, but I could do beans

Slide – a bath of baked beans. A younger ROB is sitting in it and his brother is pushing it down a hill. They're screaming with delight.

or something, or toast.'

'I'll be alright.' He touches my shoulder as he walks past and we never touch and he notices how cold I am.

'Shall I put the heating on, you're cold.'

'No, it's okay, I just got a bit wet earlier, my T-shirt's still wet, I'll change in a minute.'

'You should change now.' Me and my brother

Slide – brother.

have this weird competitive thing about who mothers who… Not in a… Neither of us are good at it.

'Yeah, okay,' and I walk to my room to search for a clean T-shirt (generally I keep my washing down the side of my bed of in a laundry basket) and I'm crying slightly I realise as I peel off my clothes, I peel off to completely naked and I just stand there, and I look down at myself and I'm all red and blotchy. I sit on my bed for a minute, I put on Eva Cassidy on the CD (it's in there already actually – I just press play and I'd have listened to Jay-Z if he was in there – it's just Eva is normally my wank music, if I think my brother can hear me wanking, I put on a CD, generally Eva Cassidy, because it doesn't distract me – it might be because she's dead), and listen to 'Fields of Gold' for a little bit, which doesn't have the most coherent lyric in the world, or at least I don't understand it, and then I get dressed and turn off Eva, and go back out to my brother.

'Okay?' he says, and he's putting bread in the toaster. A toaster which burns most things now because the filaments (is that the right term?) are knackered because we've never emptied it (my brother says if we did empty it now it'd properly knacker it so he'd prefer to just leave it and I could buy a new toaster if I wanted one, and I've never brought it up again).

'You sure you don't want a shower?'

'I'll warm up first.'

'That might warm you up.'

'No.'

'You look tired.'

And then I started crying. His back was turned to me and I felt a tear roll out, and then another one, and I tried to walk out of the room but he saw me before I left and followed me. With a sort of 'wha… come back, come back. What's the matter?' I mean, both him and me are terrible at this kind of… Though I'd be better than he is.

I walked straight up the stairs and locked myself in the bathroom. He was straight behind me but I locked it before he had a chance to stop me. Our bathroom

Slides – a series of slides of the inside of a grotty bachelory bathroom.

is a mess, and it's cold because we leave the window open all the time, and it doesn't smell as a result and it's not horrible, it's a mess in terms of too many toothpastes and too many toothbrushes and old and new razors and a mirror that's never been washed and scuzz in the bath. But it's my brother's

Slide – brother.

job to clean it.

He knocks on the door. 'Let me in, Rob.'

Slide – Rob.

I don't say anything. I actually hold my breath, which is a hard job when you're crying which seems to require more breath for some reason. I don't cry very often though.

'I've just got a headache,' I say, and I did, and had all day, I always get one when I haven't slept or had hardly slept. I can keep going, I have good adrenalin, which is why I think it hits me harder, because my body is either on 'go' or 'stop' whereas most people when they're tired act tired.

'Listen,' he's thinking, you can always tell when he's thinking, 'I'm going to go down and turn out the oven and when I come back up you can be out, or you can be in but I'm going to stay out here, so think about it, okay?' You can tell he's a manager. My parents always say that, they don't get that actually their idea of what a manager is, like a white collar, isn't what he is. I mean, they don't understand that. We're both a disappointment really, but they won't admit that. My dad'd

Slide – Dad.

never fucking admit it, he'd rather take another brick to a dog actually.

Slide – bloodied dog, lying in the middle of a cul-de-sac.

He goes off downstairs and I clean my teeth quickly, I love cleaning my teeth, he always tells me off for flossing in front of the TV, and then I turn on the shower. But I don't get in.

He knocks again. 'I'm back.'

He knocks again. 'I can hear you're not in the shower, okay, mate.'

He bangs on the door. 'I'm worried. Come on. You could be doing anything in there.'

Slide – a dancing girl doing 'anything'.

'Relax,' I shout, I turn off the shower, clean my teeth again and unlock the door as I do, with the toothbrush in my mouth.

He opens it quickly and relaxes. 'What's going on?'

'Nothing.' I wash my face. 'I'm just tired, I didn't get much sleep last night.'

'Yeah,' he puts his hand up so it's on the top of the door and then almost swings on it, 'I was going to ask about that, where did you get to you, dirty stop-out?' He laughs. I wash my face again. 'Shall we talk about it? Did she hit you or bite you

Slide – dog.

or something?' He laughs again.

'I'm fine.'

'No. You're not.'

'I'm fine, alright? I opened the door, I'm not hurting myself.'

'Okay.' He sniffs hard then, gets up a lot of phlegm, spits in the sink and then washes it down. 'Will you come downstairs, and I'll finish the pizza

Slide – half a pizza.

and you can eat. You need to eat.' I follow him downstairs and it's not that I don't think about it – what I've done – but I don't think about it as much.

We eat pizza and beans on toast

Slide – boys and the bath of beans.

almost in silence whilst watching an episode of *Will & Grace*
(my brother

Slide – brother.

is really really into *Will & Grace*, oddly-oddly over-the-toply
into it). But, also oddly, we're sitting by each other on the sofa.
He told me to sit on it, when we came downstairs, and so I did
and he went into the kitchen to finish dinner, and then he came
back out again, put his food down, cleared the side of the sofa
beside me and sat down on it. It didn't feel terrible and it wasn't
like we'd never done it before, my mum

Slide – Mum.

came up for a week a few months ago (to do shopping she said,
but actually she wanted to clean her house) and we'd had to sit
by each other a few times then but most of the time our mum
sat on the sofa with one of us and the other sat on the greasy
chair. But it did feel weird, the sofa wasn't huge so our hips
almost touched, do you know what I mean? We don't talk any
more after that, but we seem to keep watching the TV for ages.

He was pretty irrelevant when we were younger, my brother
was. It's funny, because now he's quite central. I don't know
why. He is quite like my dad. When my sister died, they were
both the same. Like 'How do we do the right thing, how can we
make this better?' whilst hidden behind a sofa. Do you know
what I mean? He was a dick.

There's nothing worse than waking up on your brother's lap,

Slide – brother.

particularly as I was pretty sure he had an erection.

*Slide – brother, this time naked, in his hands he holds a giant
erection.*

So I got up as sharply as I could considering I had a broken
neck as a result of sleeping with my head at an angle of 66
degrees. I actually never sleep well unless I'm in my own bed

on my own, so waking up on my brother's lap on a cheap, small and greasy sofa was pretty unbelievable. Second night on a sofa too, which is odd. I have a mouthful of what has turned from phlegm into what feels like pus. Anyway, I remembered pretty quickly, not that it stopped me (should it have stopped me, I think we're back into whether remorse is a worthwhile emotion, which I'm not sure it is), I eat Weetabix,

Slide – 'WITH-A-BIX'.

I should shower but I don't, and this is two sticky sex sessions later and I leave my brother

Slide – brother, again naked.

asleep. I don't know what woke me up to be honest, maybe it was the erection, I had one too which makes matters worse, I haven't dribbled in his lap anyway.

I eat Weetabix

Slide – 'WITH-A-BIX'.

sitting in the greasy chair and I'm only about three metres from his face as I do and he doesn't wake up so I leave him asleep, Blockbuster can cope. I actually put the Weetabix spoon on to his torso, to see whether he was really asleep, but he doesn't wake up. So I just leave that too.

I half expect Jason

Slide – Jason. Small, ginger, camp, adorable.

to say something as I walk to my desk but he doesn't, he's monitoring a call (probably Shirley's).

Slide – Shirley. Desperate, greasy, mid-thirties and hates being so.

They're all on calls, Tom

Slide – Tom, mid-twenties, cool but not attractive.

looks surprised to see me but winks, Debbie

Slide – Debbie, mid-thirties, suits it better than Shirley. Attractive in a Meryl Streep-type way.

waves, in a very flirty way, that also was a new thing, she'd been talking to me all week and sending me stuff, and yesterday she'd been weird too. Although I left at lunchtime. And Shirley

Slide – Shirley. The slide-changer start making more noise again.

looks at Debbie

Slide – Debbie.

as she does and everything seems normal. I plug in my headset before I turn my computer on, you're supposed to have your computer up and running but they pay you from the time you plug your headset in so everyone does that first and then bullshits any call they get, writing down the caller's BAN number (sort of a reference number) and the exact details of their problem which is all stuff we normally do anyway while the computer loads and then explaining some boring protocol while you type everything in. Or –

'Vodafone Connect customer services?' And this is the first time I've spoken and the pus is still there and has mixed with the Weetabix.

'Do I give you – what is this – a B-A-N?' An old person, my favourites. Their problems are easy, which is probably a parable for something far wider. They're brilliant to deal with in the morning because they don't mind time passing – most of them are grateful for it. And when the problem is solved they think you're a genius and sometimes they write in, which means brownie points, sometimes I even suggest they write in. Tom

Slide – Tom.

hates them, he likes serious problems, Shirley

Slide – Shirley.

and Debbie

Slide – Debbie.

both like men, I like old people.

*Slide – hardcore 'grey' porn. An eighty-year-old woman
being fucked by a twenty-year-old stud.*

We should transfer calls between ourselves, divide the labour.

'That's right, or your mobile phone number.'

'Well, I've got the B-A-N in front of me. Shall I give it you?'
He says it like it's a swear word.

'Yes please.'

'492 – '

'Can you give me the number above?' I interrupt.

'Oh. That's right. 1349674313.' I write it down, my computer's
not up yet, but do you see what I mean about time passing?

'Okay, so that's 1349674313.'

'That's right. Have you got my details now?'

'What can I help you with?' I don't pull it off but he can't
question me yet.

'It doesn't seem to be turning on.'

'How long have you had the phone, Mr…' I realise I have no
idea what his name is and my computer has stopped turning
itself on, so I restart it. I am sweating but it's sort of calm sweat.

'Thompson. Do you not have it on screen?'

'Yes. Sorry. How long have you had it, Mr Thompson?'

'Does it not say so on screen? At least two years.'

'This computer was incorrectly shut down so we're now
scanning the C-Drive for errors.' Thank you.

'Right. And what have you tried, to get it turned on, Mr
Thompson?'

'Well. Nothing other than pressing the button. It's pay-and-go, I
only use it for emergencies.'

'But it's fully charged.'

'Oh yes, I tried charging it.'

'Great. What type of phone is it, Mr Thompson?' The screen finally comes up,

Slide – a computer screen loaded up.

I log in and bash in his BAN.

Debbie.

Slide – Debbie.

ICMs 'I liked your text,'

Slide – 'I liked your text'.

ROB turns around and looks at it, he's confused.

she says.

'Oh, I don't know, well, Motorola, it's black.'

I ICM back '?????'

Slide – '?????'

'Can you take the back cover off for me, Mr Thompson?' I wipe my forehead, it's sticky sweat, if you know what I mean, like I've got hair gel in, which I haven't, I just need to wash my hair. But Debbie

Slide – Debbie.

doesn't notice. She looks across at me, she's on a call, she hammers at her keys, she doesn't ever type properly, she hammers, it's like she resents the keyboard for denying her fingernails (she asked Jason

Slide – Jason.

for one of those machines you can dictate to so that she didn't have to type, but he said (a) that would be ridiculously expensive and (b) it wouldn't work in a call centre, it'd try and write down everything – you see what I mean about him? He has thorough thoughts, I always go with the first thought in my head, Jason thinks things through, he's probably the person, at the moment, I most respect in my entire life, and, if I'm honest, he's pretty thick, he's just thorough, which I think is a hugely underrated quality).

'It won't come off, it seems not to come off. I won't break it, will I?'

'No, there should be a button up the top of the back, press that and slide it off.'

'The text you sent me yesterday, you're not going to get me to repeat it.'

Slide – 'The text you sent me yesterday, you're not going to get me to repeat it ;-))))'.

Her ICM slides on to my screen. All the time drawling Essex-girl spiel into her headset, trying to advise some customer that he's been cut off for non-payment. I didn't send her a text yesterday, I phoned though, I think. She's pushing out her tits again. She rubs one of the buttons of her blouse with her platinum ring. Debbie

Slide – Debbie.

didn't know ICMs were viewable by the moderator – like our calls – otherwise she wouldn't have done any of it. But for me, the great advantage of being massively over-qualified for your job is that you can afford to lose it.

'That's right. Right. There's a big battery underneath.'

'Can you take that out?' I dislodge a large piece of pussy Weetabix

Slide – 'WITH-A-BIX'.

which had sort of hidden itself in my wisdom teeth which are sort of coming through and are still very tender, it almost makes me puke anyway.

'How does this come out?'

'Just pull it out, Mr Thompson.'

'How am I supposed to pull it out? I'd rather not break it.'

'It won't break it.' Debbie

Slide – Debbie.

finishes her call and turns to look at me, she sucks in her cheeks and giggles. I don't know what that means. Stacy

Slide – Stacy.

does that too. I presume it's a code, but... 'Fine.' He's getting angry now. 'Do I start at the top or the bottom to take it out.'

'Just take it out, Mr Thompson.' I raise my voice slightly.

'No!' He shouts.

Jason

Slide – Jason.

smoothly interrupts the call. 'Mr Thompson? My name's Jason Gould, I'm Rob's

Slide – ROB.

ROB *turns around to look at it. He's entirely confused, he wipes his forehead.*

line manager, if you see the springs are up the top of the phone – it's a Motorola 1133 according to our system – so if you just push towards the springs, push the battery towards the springs then it should just flick out.'

I disconnect from the call. And just sit there. Shirley

Slide – Shirley.

sidles past, she touches my shoulder 'Jenny.

Slide – Jenny, the picture has been taken far too close to her face. She's older than ROB, and not as attractive, but she's smiling. She has 'BLIND DATE' written on her forehead.

was asking after you, you know. Anyone else want a coffee?' she says.

Debbie

Slide – Debbie.

looks across at me – 'Shirley,

Slide – Shirley.

he's not interested in her, she's a dog.'

Slide – dog with his brains bashed out is lying in the middle of the cul-de-sac.

Slide – a number of shots zoom in, like crime-scene photos: an old man is holding a torch and a bloodied brick; he has the brick poised above the dog's head, he's waiting for the dog to show signs of life.

Jason

Slide – Jason.

puts his call on hold, he's angry. 'Can you not talk like that please Debbie.'

Slide – Debbie.

He sounds like John Inman

Slide – John Inman.

Slide – Hugh Grant.

Slide – a pretty little girl sitting in a coffin, playing a game.

with his 'Debbie.'

Slide – Debbie.

'I'm on a call, as is Tom.'

Slide – Tom.

Tom waves his hand as if to say I don't give a fuck. So we all sit there in silence.

'You look rough,' Jason

Slide – Jason.

says softly, when he disconnects from his (my) call. I mean, Debbie is flirting because she's bored probably, but I do feel sick. 'You sure you're okay?'

'Yeah.'

'Switch your computer on before you plug in next time, okay?' he says.

'Yeah.'

'Leave him alone, Jason,' Debbie

Slide – Debbie.

says. They had an affair once, Debbie is happily engaged by the way, but anyway, Jason

Slide – Jason.

had been keener on it than her. She hadn't got to Tom

Slide – Tom.

yet. Or me, properly. 'No, this is my job. Sorry Rob,

Slide – ROB.

there was a memo, switch your computer on first.'

'Okay.'

'You had the right instincts about that caller, you just need to take it slower with the older callers.'

'I know.'

'Are you okay, Rob?'

Slide – a child standing on a chair, singing his heart out.

Jason

Slide – Jason.

asks. Debbie

Slide – Debbie.

starts hammering into her computer again.

'Yeah.'

'We need to talk.' Debbie ICMs.

Slide – 'WE need to talk.'

'Come to the cloakroom NOW.'

Slide – 'COME TO THE CLOAKROOM NOW.' Then another slide with the same lettering on a red backdrop. Then blue backdrop.

Complete with the campness of the capital letters as well.

He turns to look at it. It changes to a yellow backdrop.

And she looks at me, and picks up her bag and she leaves. Her shirt is too tight and I'm not sure she's wearing a bra and she postures away to the cloakroom. One of the functions of the ICM is that you can forward the same message on and it will only show its original sender – Debbie – I don't know why it does that. So I forward it on and I watch, and Jason

Slide – Jason.

looks worried and then goes to the cloakroom and Tom

Slide – Tom.

laughs and does fuck all and this guy from accounts walks past at great speed and Shirley

Slide – Shirley.

follows him. And I disconnect and leave the office. Tom

Slide – Tom.

watches me go though. Or at least that's how I remember it, and it feels like I'm remembering it at the time, things are sliding out all the time.

He gets up, he walks to the front of the stage, then he stops, scratches his bollocks and laughs.

I catch the tram home and I don't buy a ticket but I'm not caught. There's still quite a few commuters around but they all get off at East Croydon station so I'm quite worried I'll be stopped on the short bit up to Lebanon Road. But I'm not. My brother's

Slide – brother.

gone by the time I get in so he obviously woke up on time too. Perhaps he was awake this morning and faked it out, I can't imagine we'd have had much to say. I've got this thing where I pace around the house and I always stick to the same route: up the stairs, along the corridor and back, down the stairs, through the living room, circle the kitchen and I'm sure I look like the Rain Man but it does calm me down. I look on the internet, check my favourite sites. But that's not that good either today.

I try and ring Stacy

Slide – Stacy, but it takes too long coming up.

from the phone in the house rather than my mobile (I don't think she's got my house-phone number stored) but she keeps her mobile switched off at work. She was the one I'd normally talk to, so that was sort of automatic rather than anything else. I try and ring Debbie

Slide – Debbie.

too but she's switched off too, Debbie rings back whenever you call her whether or not you leave a message, she goes through all her missed calls and rings them back, she's very sweet like that, so I don't leave a message, and I'm not going to leave one on Stacy's,

Slide – Stacy.

because I need to get that from new. I wonder whether to ring my brother,

Slide – brother.

but I don't actually have that much to say to him. Then Debbie

Slide – Debbie.

actually does ring, my mobile (when I'd been calling from the house phone) but I disconnect it.

Then the police ring the doorbell (which seems wrong to me, policemen should knock on the door, it's much more action-hero).

And I…

You see, my problem is that I've always worried too much about tomorrow – I save up too much and I never spend – I've always not watched a video or something I've just bought or recorded because I want to save it for when I really want to watch it. Then I end up not watching it at all, because I've gone off it. I think I'll really really want to watch it tomorrow, but I end up not wanting to, and I laugh about that sometimes. My brother, if he's got it, wants to watch it straight away. I save money 'for tomorrow', I've got so much money saved and I could do this or that, I could buy a computer, or go travelling, but I keep working at Vodafone and I make a profit off that, taking away my living expenses, I still make about £400 a month on top of everything I have to pay for, because I work shitloads of overtime.

Slide – Stacy, finally it's a different shot, it's her masturbating last night in their temporarily shared bed. We can also see a fretful ROB *peering over her and wondering what to do.*

I'm quite tired and I worry too much about tomorrow, and I think Stacy (*He turns to look at her and then turns back to the audience*.) – well...

I'm crying again when I answer the door. I'm trying to smile too though.

Slide – ROB *on the phones at Vodafone. He is laughing at a joke that Tom has told.*

ROB *waits a moment then walks out through the audience. He walks quickly.*

2nd MAY 1997

For Laura Wade

'What the electorate gives, the electorate can take away'
Tony Blair

2nd May 1997 was first produced by nabokov and the Bush Theatre in association with Watford Palace Theatre and Mercury Theatre, Colchester, at the Bush Theatre, London, on 8 September 2009, with the following cast:

JAKE	James Barrett
ROBERT	Geoffrey Beevers
MARIE	Linda Broughton
WILL	Jamie Samuel
IAN	Hugh Skinner
SARAH	Phoebe Waller-Bridge

Director	George Perrin
Designer	Hannah Clark
Lighting Designer	Philip Gladwell
Sound Designer	Emma Laxton

The play subsequently toured to Watford Palace Theatre, Mercury Theatre, Colchester, and the Royal Exchange Theatre, Manchester.

Characters

ROBERT, *seventy-one*
MARIE, *sixty-four*
SARAH, *twenty-eight*
IAN, *twenty-nine*
JAKE, *eighteen*
WILL, *eighteen*

PART ONE

11.38 p.m.

The simple yet textured bedroom of a cultured older couple.

ROBERT *sits up in a slightly grand bed, looking at a small packet of photos; seventy-ish and handsome, he is wearing reading glasses. There is an oxygen cylinder beside his bed. He's calling offstage.*

ROBERT. So which one's this and why's she in a bikini?

He flicks to another photo.

And this one – this one's new. I recognise him. But I don't know where from. He's not the new one, is he?

He continues to flick.

MARIE *(from off)*. No. The new one wasn't with her. They were all just friends...

ROBERT. They seem to have – well, he's certainly touching her, not – I'm never sure what touching is friendly any more. But that I wouldn't say was...

If I'd have touched Mary Watson like that, I'd have been slapped.

MARIE *is in the ensuite bathroom. She is making quite a lot of noise in there, working her new electric toothbrush.*

MARIE *(she stays off)*. Mary Watson?

ROBERT. Mary? I must have told you. Mary? First – well, first something. She let me hold hands with her once, and then said I was too clammy – said my hands felt like goose grease. I realised then – if she could afford goose in her house – well, no chance for me. I don't know why I'm remembering her.

Mary? Do I mean Mary Watson? Maybe it was Phillips. You'd remember her name better than I, and I'd have surely told you... Maybe it wasn't Mary.

Do you hear that? The bells of Alzheimer's. The bells. The bells. Remembering –

Bikini.

Bikini.

MARIE. You do not have Alzheimer's...

ROBERT. There's about twenty shots of this girl in a bikini. Same – bikini – well, some – no, same bikini, just different angle. More of a – bottom one –

Bikini.

Bikini.

MARIE. She's just trying to keep us involved, darling...

ROBERT. Funny way to stay involved, to show us lots of shots of this girl's bottom.

He turns a photo through ninety degrees in his hands – he raises his eyebrow in surprise.

MARIE. She thought we'd want to see them.

ROBERT. But they're not of anything, well, not of –

MARIE. Then put them back in the envelope and finish your speech.

He thinks, and then continues flicking through.

ROBERT. A few landscapes. A spot of nature wouldn't be... People on a beach in their pants – touching each other... and 'clubbing'. There are some of 'clubbing'. Did I tell you about the 'clubbing ones'? Most of them seem to be wearing bikinis in those too – bikinis and sunglasses indoors.

MARIE. It was a holiday, Robert. Not a fact-finding mission.

ROBERT. Oh. Yes. Not that – facts. I firmly disagree with the notion that facts and entertainment are somehow different entities.

He turns over to another picture.

Tweedledum and Tweedledee called from the office.

MARIE. What did they want?

ROBERT. And they're hideously small. These photos.

MARIE. You buy an extra packet for a pound. It's one of those you send off for. But they come in that size.

ROBERT. Well. They're very small.

MARIE *enters the room and smiles at her husband. She is sixty-ish, stylish, careful; she's wearing a face mask.*

MARIE. Large enough for you to make out a bikini, though...

ROBERT *looks at her and smiles.*

ROBERT. Yes.

MARIE. Which is surprising because it is not a large bikini.

She smiles and exits for the bathroom again.

He puts down the photos. He picks up a pad and a pen. He looks at them.

ROBERT. They said there's a race on. Tweedlewotsits. The office did. First to declare. Sunderland. Hamilton. Somewhere else. They thought they'd have the first results within the hour.

MARIE (*she stays off*). Maybe we should have the goggleometer on then.

ROBERT. No. No. We'll have quite enough of that later.

He coughs, touches his chest, and then looks around regally. He puts down the pad and the paper with deliberate grace. He thinks for something to do, sighs and picks up the pictures again. He holds them but doesn't look.

Besides, it's Dimbleby versus Dimbleby again tonight. Bored silly with raised eyebrows on one side? Why not change channels and be bored equally silly by the younger and less successful brother? ITV was set up to provide competition, you know.

MARIE. I think he's quite attractive.

ROBERT. David?

MARIE. Jonathan. He has a much kinder face than David. And a slightly grubby smile.

ROBERT. I'd give it to the black man. The – Trevor – you know, the 'And finally…'

MARIE. McDonald.

ROBERT. They said – the office said – 'Nine cabinet members will fall' in their slightly portentous voices…

MARIE. Which one was it? George or…?

ROBERT. You know I don't like it when you call them by their real names…

MARIE. Tweedledum or…?

ROBERT. I have no idea. They're much of a muchness. To be honest with you, there's been once or twice I've almost called them Tweedledum and Tweedledee. 'Nine cabinet members will fall.' No sympathy. Mild excitement in their voices. Moist excitement.

MARIE. Do they know which ones will…?

ROBERT. They said – they told me they wanted to talk to me about 'future opportunities'.

MARIE. I hope you laughed at them.

ROBERT. They've rung about twice during the entire campaign. You don't laugh at crumbs.

MARIE. You *do* laugh at *them*, though.

ROBERT. Norman always thought I'd make a good lord.

MARIE. Norman was flirting with you…

ROBERT *looks off, not exactly surprised at that, but surprised at her tone.*

He turns back to the photos.

ROBERT. Well.

I have no idea who any of them are… in these photos…

MARIE. Hannah's friends.

ROBERT. Yes. I know they're Hannah's friends. But – I'm still not…

MARIE. The girl in the bikini is Kaylee. You know her…

ROBERT. Kaylee? I thought she wore glasses.

He looks more carefully at a photo, he adjusts his own glasses.

MARIE *comes back into the room, the face mask now washed off.*

He smiles at her.

Didn't she – wear glasses…?

She sits on the bed.

She takes the photos from him.

She flicks through and starts pointing out important things.

MARIE. These are the two – Laura and Cherry – she's renting the flat with… and this one's the one who had the problem with the dead dog, Terry –

ROBERT. The one who got her the interview… Well, we like him.

MARIE. And this one's the one who made the silly mistake with the overdose, Kirsty… and this one's that one that wasn't very nice to her, Phil.

ROBERT. Wasn't he?

MARIE. Phil. Second year at Manchester. He told her he loved her, and then found a better bet. When she had the issue with the eating.

He remembers the issue with the eating.

ROBERT. Him?

MARIE. He's nice enough. Just a little confused. Confused Phil.

ROBERT. And why was she on holiday with Confused Phil? Was she confused? He's not the one touching her inappropriately, is he?

MARIE. He's nice enough. Besides, he's in her friendship group, she didn't want to – I think 'alienate' is the word she used.

She smiles at him. He looks at her with a gentle frown.

ROBERT. I didn't think the 'lord' thing was…

She kisses his cheek.

MARIE. I know you didn't.

He pats the bed.

ROBERT. Are you getting in?

MARIE *laughs.*

MARIE. Bikini got your heart racing, is it?

ROBERT *laughs and then coughs.*

ROBERT. No. I didn't mean…

MARIE. No. I know.

MARIE *gets up and opens the wardrobe, she begins to pull out things from inside.*

You tell Tweedledum and Tweedledee that you're very grateful for their interest, but if you're out then you're staying out…

ROBERT *coughs again.*

ROBERT. And shaking it all about.

MARIE. Well, then, tell them what you like…

ROBERT. They're just trying to make the best of a bad egg.

MARIE. They've thrown the bad egg away.

ROBERT *scratches his neck, so as to avoid any telling facial expression.*

ROBERT. Maybe I should take her on holiday...

MARIE. Who?

ROBERT. Hannah. There's plenty she should see. I could show her there's more to life than beaches and 'clubbing'.

MARIE. She's not your next project.

ROBERT. I didn't say that.

MARIE. You could take me on holiday.

ROBERT. I intend to.

ROBERT *coughs.*

Then coughs again.

Then coughs repeatedly.

Then takes a breath.

MARIE *looks at him carefully and turns on the oxygen cylinder.*

She gestures the mask towards him.

MARIE. Are you...?

ROBERT *pushes the mask away, and opens a drawer and pulls out a clean handkerchief.*

He holds it to his mouth as he coughs again.

Then coughs again and again and again.

Then he stops.

He takes the oxygen mask from her and takes two distinct breaths.

Would you like some water?

ROBERT. No.

He checks his handkerchief.

MARIE. Blood?

ROBERT. Only a little.

She exits to the bathroom, pours a glass of water and comes back in with it.

She hands it to him. He takes another two breaths from the mask and takes a sip.

He hands her back the mask, she turns off the oxygen.

MARIE. What has Dr Phillips been saying about…?

ROBERT. He hasn't.

He takes another sip of his water.

They're just trying to support a man who has had his seat taken from him –

MARIE. They're dusting the cornices…

ROBERT. In – well, two hours' time. Three hours' time, I'm out of a job, they're…

MARIE. They don't want you saying anything disrespectful in your speech.

ROBERT *is starting to flush up.*

ROBERT. That's not what – I worked hard for these people, for this Party, a little reward. A – little – reward…

MARIE. If you get worked up like this, you'll start coughing again.

ROBERT. You work me up. You're working me up. They made very clear – compensations would be… They do not call very often, when they do call, it is clear, I should listen to what they have to say, crumbs are… They wanted to talk to me about my future. This is a good thing. Yet, you don't seem…

He coughs.

You don't seem the slightest bit interested. You don't think I should take my daughter away, you don't think –

MARIE. I think you should take me away.

ROBERT (*impassioned*). *I will not* – simply – *fill* my time.

> *Beat.* MARIE *looks at him, and acknowledges him, like a woman acknowledges a man she loves – but she doesn't concede.*

MARIE. I know you won't.

> MARIE *walks over to the wardrobe. She picks out two dresses, and then holds them up against herself.*

> This, or this? Hannah says the brown one shows off my figure better.

ROBERT. You wore that to the constituency barbecue.

MARIE. Did I?

ROBERT. Where's the black one with a pattern?

MARIE. How do you remember what I wore to the barbecue?

ROBERT. You spilt something on it. I had to get it dry-cleaned. You looked pretty in it. Who knows what I remember...? I seem to be remembering Mary... what was her name? Goose fat. I really think her name was Mary. I remember it being similar to your name.

MARIE. I'll take that as a compliment.

ROBERT. Take it as you like for who you like for what you like.

> *The phone begins to ring.*

> MARIE *looks at* ROBERT.

> It's too early yet...

> MARIE *exits.*

> ROBERT *coughs and then coughs.*

> *He touches his chest. He allows himself a look of pain.*

> *He picks up the photographs again. He looks through them.*

> *He laughs.*

Now there's a profit.

Barely two strips of material.

Still, if it works for her.

It certainly… Marie? Marie… Oh.

He'd forgotten she was on the phone.

He looks at the pad and the pen.

He takes off his glasses. He puts them on the bedside cabinet.

He swings his legs over the side of the bed, breathes and then stands up.

He takes a breath, wobbles slightly, and sits back on the bed.

He looks around.

He stands again. Walks determinedly forward, wobbles.

Fuck.

And then crumples. To the ground.

Fuck.

He attempts to stop his fall, he attempts to move back towards the bed. He accomplishes neither. He lands harder than feels right. He coughs and then coughs again.

Fuck.

He laughs.

(*Faux voice.*) 'Nine cabinet members will fall.'

He laughs again.

Stupid fucking pricks.

He coughs and then coughs repeatedly.

He holds his hand over his mouth.

He looks at his hand and then smears it over his pyjamas.

The bloodstain stays where it is.

He looks around the room.

He pulls himself over to the wall.

He tries to get traction.

He tries to pull himself up.

He fails.

MARIE *comes in the room.*

She looks at him.

She looks at him a long, long time; he smiles at her.

MARIE. Bit of a...

ROBERT. The problem came when I decided to dance.

MARIE *laughs.*

Then looks at him a bit longer.

MARIE. Do you want...?

ROBERT. No.

MARIE. That was Hannah. She wanted to wish you good luck.

ROBERT. Did she?

MARIE. I told her you didn't need luck. You were a Tony target seat.

ROBERT. Twenty-two. I'm twenty-two. Target seat twenty-two.

MARIE. You don't need luck, you need Armageddon.

ROBERT. Am I – covered up...?

MARIE. You've a bloodstain on your left thigh.

ROBERT. Little John. I can't see if Little John is showing his head.

MARIE. No... No.

She smiles.

No. I don't know why it would matter to you. But no... Nor Robin Hood.

ROBERT. I always – Brighton bomb – and my abiding memory – was Norman on the television being dragged from the rubble – in his pyjamas – a man that really shouldn't have survived, and he was trying –

He starts laughing.

– this great moment – this greatest – defiant –'Listen to me, IRA, you will not disturb our Government, our Norman Tebbit can survive everything you throw at him' – and then you realised, then you realised, everyone realised watching him – the news cameras watching him – that he was desperately – trying desperately to cover his testicles up because his pyjama trousers had been ripped by the blast.

MARIE *is not laughing.*

MARIE *thinks and then moves towards him, but she doesn't help him up, instead she slowly gets on the floor.*

She lies down beside him.

They say nothing.

Will you light me a cigarette?

MARIE *thinks, and then sits up and takes a packet of cigarettes from the bedside drawer – she doesn't stand up, just leans across for them, lights the cigarette, takes a few puffs, and then puts it into* ROBERT's *mouth. She stays sitting up. He stays lying down.*

I was thinking – this evening – for my – speech –

MARIE. Your – you finished…?

ROBERT. ….nothing – too – Secret is, not to get on TV when you lose as – someone told me – may have been Willie – no, I was thinking what I considered my greatest achievements. I was making – a list. In my head.

She leans against the door.

MARIE. In your head?

ROBERT. It wasn't a long list.

MARIE. You haven't started it yet, have you?

He looks at her, irritated. She smiles, trying to swallow her irritation. And rubs her arm.

ROBERT. It wasn't a... And the events seemed so – I resolved the pensions problem when British Gas privatised.

MARIE. You were always great at the detail of things...

ROBERT. I did some important work restructuring the prisons subsection of the Home Office. Work people were grateful for – but significant – I was always good at the detail of things...

MARIE. Great at the detail of things...

ROBERT. Pennies. Pounds. Never headlines.

MARIE. Who needs headlines?

Pause. ROBERT *takes the cigarette from his mouth and hands it to* MARIE, *who smokes some of it.*

ROBERT. Do you know a man I always admired – Roy Jenkins...

MARIE. Roy Jenkins? That's a leap.

ROBERT. Not – I didn't agree with anything he did –

MARIE. Roy... Jenkins?

ROBERT. Didn't concern himself with the ladder. If they didn't like him, he'd dazzle them...

MARIE. He was just as ambitious as the rest of you. More so.

ROBERT. And the things he got done. As Home Secretary: legalisation of abortion, legalisation of homosexuality, abolition of the death penalty –

MARIE. Sounds like a shopping list for Sodom and Gomorrah –

ROBERT. No one wanted, Wilson was a... But he worked at it – abortion – back-door work – excuse the –

MARIE *puts the cigarette back into* ROBERT*'s mouth.*

MARIE. Abortions. Sodom and Gomorrah –

ROBERT. He looked down the private members' bill list – told them he'd make sure they'd have time on the floor if they supported one of his measures. Hey presto. He hooked David Steel. Steel got all the credit, but it was Roy...

MARIE. I don't think there's any credit involved.

ROBERT *is flushing again*.

ROBERT. Then Europe. The Labour Party then hated the idea of – far more angry about it than we are now... Roy got the 'Yes' vote, Roy got us in.

MARIE. Ted was the one who... Not that there's any –

ROBERT. Without Roy he'd have never succeeded. That hung on a knife edge, it was Roy... Never Prime Minister, but the changes he made... The changes he made...

MARIE. He was Home Secretary. He was Chancellor. You did your job.

ROBERT. He did great things. He – found – mountains to move. And I think what I – did – didn't –

MARIE. Calm – slow down –

ROBERT. He changed lives – here – there – fucking everywhere –

MARIE. I don't like it when you swear –

ROBERT. And I sorted out the pensions black hole in a –

MARIE. Robert. Please.

ROBERT (*fully full*). I did nothing. I look back on – I should have been. I wasn't, and I should have been a – great man. I always thought I'd be a great man, and I wasn't. I just – wasn't.

Beat.

He makes a yelping noise.

Beat.

He makes half a yelping noise.

Beat. MARIE *doesn't look at him. Then she does. Then she doesn't again.*

MARIE. David Steel bought me a white wine spritzer once. I was wearing the red dress with the legs. I tried to decline it, but he was very persistent. You were talking to – someone – or waiting to – he seemed less inclined to talk to anyone. He kept telling me it was only half wine, so it didn't count.

Roy was a nasty piece of lechery too. Sodom and Gomorrah. He'd have fitted in. Party hands.

Beat. MARIE *pulls a pillow down from the bed and puts it behind* ROBERT.

She then reaches further for a pillow for her. She puts it behind her head.

MARIE. Do you remember the first seat we tried for…?

ROBERT. Winchester.

MARIE. And for some reason – I was sitting at the back – for some reason you spent the entire meeting looking at me.

ROBERT. That probably was a mistake.

MARIE. Staring at me and only me. You were nervous.

ROBERT. I was petrified. I vomited three times in the toilets at Reading Station.

MARIE. And I reassured you. Looking at me reassured you.

ROBERT. It always did.

MARIE. And that was – the most wonderful – the most wonderful thing… For me. But I felt this great pressure, that my nerves not show, that I was there for you, and that I had to – absorb you to be – useful. Nerves must not show. I – absorbed – for you.

Pause. She pulls herself up to sitting.

Maybe I should write your speech. Tell the Liberal Democrats that yellow washes them out and that Labour one that I think she has issues she needs to talk about with her mother. Or her father. Or possibly both.

He touches her arm. She looks at the arm. And then at the bloodstain.

It's going to take bleach to get that out.

ROBERT. Yes.

She looks at his face, carefully, as if remembering it.

MARIE. When we got here – we won – and we fitted. And, uh…

ROBERT. Yes?

Pause. She picks up his hand, and plays with the webbing between his fingers.

MARIE. When Hannah – Hannah was – when Hannah was born you were debating a bill on out-of-town shopping centres –

ROBERT. That? It was a three-line whip and they'd suspended – the – thing – system.

MARIE. But I had my mother with me. So that was – fine.

ROBERT. I phoned as soon as I could…

MARIE. I let you listen to her breathe.

ROBERT. And then I had – to get off the line. There was a – I needed to be back in the chamber –

Pause.

MARIE. And you told me – you told me 'well done'. You said: 'I have to go now, Marie, but well done.'

Then Hannah had a few troubles settling down at night and you told me that we weren't to have any more kids, because your schedule didn't allow for it, and I let you do that. Then we sent her to St Mary's at an age where I didn't think she was ready, but you thought it'd be good for her as it was a – great – school… I wanted to go back to work, and you said that – I couldn't. You said I should come and be a secretarial support – well, I tried that, but I didn't like how you treated me. Like a secretary-wife, not a wife any more, not a – wife.

So most days – most days I took to either filling with a letter to Hannah or the radio or filling with – groups and… And I'm not much of a joiner-in. So eventually I just – waited for you.

I did my keep-fit when that started on breakfast television, but mostly I waited for you to come home. I always just – because you, because we – ever since you were that young man with the strange smile who couldn't talk to me in church. Ever since then.

Beat. She's remembering things now.

When Hannah got sick –

ROBERT. Marie –

MARIE. The first night in hospital – so pale and thin and – yellow. So yellow. I worried in case she breathed in too fiercely and her ribs cracked. And even she – even she –

Suddenly, her voice gets louder, goes from soft to loud in two paces.

Tweedledum or Tweedledee phoned me once – by accident – they were wanting… you. But they said, they kept me on the line, they didn't need to keep me on the line, but they clearly felt they needed to keep talking – why they thought they had to talk to – Conservative Central Office keeping MPs' wives entertained. They told me – this must have been twelve months ago – longer – Hestletine was doing something with someone and it had them concerned and they said – they said what an important person you were to them, and that to be sure to pass on that your support for John will have ramifications for… They started talking about the Hestletine ancestry and how we'd understand what it was to be humble Tories not related to Charles Dibdin and then they started explaining who Charles Dibdin was… And I said I knew who Charles Dibdin…

She turns and looks at him and then looks away. She spits the word out.

Humble. Humble.

You don't think I'm angry? I'm furious! To be thrown away like a used tissue, and not for reason of what you did, by voters who you served. Because it's time for change and 'that's politics'. You're not John Major, you never ran the Party, you never got close. Back to basics. Sleaze. You were basic. You were good. You were a good local MP, and you've always done a good job and now you're – not. And that's not fair. That's not how jobs are decided. That's not how I thought this would end.

But I will not have you feel a failure. That's not – you – I was very proud – of you. I didn't always agree with what you said, what you made me do, but I was you. I was you. We were you. I was you at the fêtes, and the visits, and the dinners, I was always proud to be you. And that's – that's – and I'm – that's that.

There is a long pause.

She can't look at him and he can't look at her.

Then the phone starts ringing.

They listen to it.

It rings for an age.

Then eventually rings off.

Who do you think?

ROBERT. Probably them. The results are getting close. They want us down at the count.

MARIE. Do you think?

ROBERT. It's about the right time.

MARIE. We'll use your chair.

ROBERT. Yes. Chair doesn't matter now.

MARIE *stands up.*

It takes her a moment, she catches her breath.

He looks at her strong back.

Do I need – to apologise?

Beat.

MARIE. No. No. You never did listen properly. No.

Beat. She doesn't turn around, she sets herself and then she does turn.

Come on, if you get up quick, I'll let you look at the girl in a bikini again before we have to get going…

She slowly, gently, helps him up.

Slowly. Slowly.

He stops halfway and takes a breath, and then, just like that, he's standing again and it's almost beautiful; she puts her hands on his waist.

There.

ROBERT. Yes. There.

MARIE. Okay?

ROBERT. Yes. Okay.

MARIE. Okay?

ROBERT. Yes. Yes.

MARIE. Okay.

Pause. He sways slightly.

ROBERT. What am I going to do?

MARIE. When?

ROBERT. Now. What am I going to – do?

MARIE. You'll do all sorts. We'll do all sorts. We'll take walks in the park, we'll buy a new cookery book and experiment with different things for dinner each night, we'll take drives down to see Hannah and take her food and check she's okay, we'll find friends to play cards with, we'll go to every constituency Party meeting, every branch meeting, we'll find programmes we want to watch together on television, we'll garden and win a rosette in the 'Town in Bloom' competition, we'll enjoy ourselves, we'll settle.

ROBERT. Settle?

MARIE. It's what old people do.

They look at each other. Then she leans in and softly kisses his lips.

ROBERT. I'm suddenly quite hungry.

MARIE. Are you?

ROBERT. Shall we get some chips? On the way to the results...

She softly smiles at him.

MARIE. If you'd like.

ROBERT. Dr Phillips wouldn't like it.

MARIE. No. He would not.

ROBERT. But I don't like Dr Phillips.

MARIE. He's a funny way about him, doesn't he?

ROBERT. He told me last time – he said: (*Nasal voice.*) 'In the interests of transparency, I should tell you, sir, I'm intending on voting Blair.'

MARIE. Right.

ROBERT. 'In the interests of transparency...'

MARIE *laughs.*

MARIE. 'In the interests of transparency...'

ROBERT. 'In the interests of transparency.'

She thinks, and then gently kisses him again, on the cheek and then the lips.

She pulls back and looks at him.

MARIE. Have you written anything? Have you anything to say?

He smiles, and shakes his head with a twinkle.

ROBERT. Maybe it doesn't matter. Maybe I'll write something in the car. Maybe – I'll sing.

Pause. She smiles.

MARIE. You were my great man.

ROBERT. Was I?

MARIE. Yes. You were.

ROBERT *thinks*.

ROBERT. Yes. Let's get chips.

Slow fade to black.

End of Part One.

PART TWO

2.41 a.m.

A tidy bedsit. SARAH *enters first, she's drunk, but not especially so you'd notice immediately.* IAN *isn't drunk.*

SARAH. Oh, it's not that messy…

IAN. It's not tidy.

SARAH. With the bed to the side…

IAN. And the sofa… there… you want to sit down?

SARAH. I want to look around.

IAN. Looking for what?

SARAH. I just want to poke…

I like people poking about my house.

I like people being intrigued.

IAN *smiles.*

IAN. Then we should have gone to yours… I could have been intrigued at [yours] –

SARAH. No, I followed you… If you had followed me we could have gone back to mine.

But I made the move, so I won a trip to your house.

She starts to poke about. IAN *looks at his hands.*

My mum used to love poking about my room – poke – poke – one time she found an old toothbrush she insisted I was using as a dildo. I was fifteen years old – she said, 'Lots of girls have very healthy sexual appetites at your age, I know I did, but it's a very confusing as well as perfectly natural time.'

IAN *laughs*. SARAH *looks at him*.

IAN. My dad just gave me a book. *Your Body and You*.

SARAH. 'It's perfectly natural, do you want to talk about it?
The dildo?' No, she called it something else. She called it
something – I can't remember – I think she may have called
it a 'sexual device'. Truth was, she'd heard about it on Radio
4 – *Woman's Hour* did dildos. Sexual devices.

But the truth also was that I had a new pair of Doc Martens
and I was proud of them and mud and shit kept getting
caught in the tread, because it was quite deep tread, so I used
a toothbrush to… True story. Bet I don't look like a woman
who used to wear Docs as a kid.

Maybe I do. Do I?

IAN. You could…

SARAH. You should have seen the toothbrush – I mean, you
must wonder what she thought I had up my fanny. The
toothbrush was… not clean. It was brown. The bristles were
brown. I mean, really quite… really quite… not nice.

IAN *isn't sure how to respond, so just smiles*.

*Pause. She continues to try and behave casually as she pokes
through his stuff. Eventually, she needs to break the silence…*

What shall I do with my coat?

IAN. Oh. Just put it anywhere.

SARAH. I hate phrases like that. 'Just put it anywhere.' I feel
like shouting at the screen – 'It's your dick, put it in her
fanny.'

*She starts to take off her shoes, they look like they've hurt
her feet.*

IAN. Do you?

SARAH. Sorry, am I being confrontational? It's a mixture of
drunkenness and fear of sex.

IAN. Right.

She gives her shoes to IAN. *Who doesn't quite know what to do with them, and so puts them down beside himself. In the centre of the room. It's an odd place for shoes. She looks at where he's put them. She looks at him. Slightly accusingly.*

SARAH. Don't worry. I'm not going to take the rest of my clothes off and hand them to you...

IAN. Not that – no.

She laughs. He doesn't know why.

SARAH. You were giving as good as you got at the party...

IAN. No. I wasn't –

SARAH. You fucking were, wideboy.

IAN. No. Was I?

SARAH. What was it you said... I can't remember how you said it... You said something about Blair being one bollock short of a mouthful.

IAN. I didn't.

SARAH. 'The thing about Tony Blair is, he's one bollock short of a mouthful.'

IAN. I think you've got me mixed up.

SARAH. 'One bollock short of a mouthful.' It's a lovely phrase. I was quite surprised at a Liberal Democrat...

IAN. I think... that was probably James.

SARAH. James?

IAN. James. Yes. James. He came with me. Wiry hair. Grey jacket.

I'm not much of a talker. You were mostly talking to him.

I was there. But you two talked.

He's not really a Liberal Democrat.

Beat. SARAH *appraises the situation.*

SARAH. And what happened to James?

IAN. Um. Well…

    He, uh… He had to go home.

    SARAH *bullet laughs and then bullet laughs again.*

SARAH. I went home with the wrong guy.

IAN. No.

SARAH (*really laughing*). I went home with the wrong guy.

IAN. It's – um – Did you?

SARAH. Jesus. Am I that drunk?

    Pause.

    James.

IAN. We work together. He's a good friend. Well. Colleague.

    Wiry hair. Grey jacket. Do you want to leave?

SARAH. Fuck no. This is exciting. This is like 'Guess Who?' but… sexual. 'Sexual Guess Who?' Awesome.

    She's staring at him quite intently.

IAN. Do you want the TV on? We could check what's –

SARAH. See how far you've lost yet…

IAN. Well. Not really about the winning.

    Not that it's about the taking part either…

    SARAH *laughs again.*

SARAH. It *was* a good party. 'Sexual Guess Who?' Who are you?

IAN. Who am I?

SARAH (*Cilla Black impression*). 'Hello number two, what's your name and where do you come from?'

IAN. Don't…

    She laughs again. He doesn't know why. Again.

SARAH. The Party party?

IAN. What?

SARAH. A Party having a party – funny when you – I thought that was funny – a Party having a party – Who was I talking about that with…? Did we talk at all?

IAN. Of course we did… we, um… we talked about the Millennium Bug.

SARAH. I only went because my friend Ruth told me free – booze… 'Come to the Party party.' It might have been her I was – talking about it with.

IAN. Yeah? Yeah. That's sort of why James came… We don't really… It's open-door. We talked about restricting, but…

SARAH. I can fit my whole fist in my mouth. Can you do that?

IAN. What? Can you?

SARAH. Sorry – party – party tricks, that's the way my brain works, I won't show you. It's painful and makes me look very unattractive.

IAN. I'm sure it doesn't.

SARAH. Well… it does…

Pause.

IAN. There was a guy at my school whose party trick was he could fit his whole penis in an eggcup.

Pause. SARAH barks a laugh and then stops.

SARAH. Jesus.

IAN. What?

SARAH. 'Hello, Cilla, my name is…'

IAN. Ian. We definitely did the names thing… You're Sarah.

SARAH. 'And I am a… Liberal Democrat, Cilla.'

IAN. Housing Officer. I'm a Housing Officer.

Pause. SARAH tries to think of a response to that. She fails. She barks another laugh.

SARAH. Have you got any alcohol?

IAN. Good idea. What would you like?

SARAH. I would like a pint of water and a large glass of red
   wine…

IAN. That… I can do…

SARAH. Good.

> IAN *exits*. SARAH *looks around his room. She picks a book
> out. Will Hutton* – The State We're In. *She flicks through. She
> smiles. She reads a page. She calls off…*

> You write notes in the margins of your books.

> IAN *reappears. Suddenly. Anxiously.*

IAN. Not really.

SARAH. You've written an exclamation mark beside a – you've
   written an exclamation mark – what does it say?

IAN. Don't read it out.

> SARAH *reads the paragraph. She reads it again. She
> frowns. She puts the book back on the shelf.*

SARAH. Do you do it for your fiction books too? Do you
   underline your fiction books? Or is it only facts – are you
   only interested in facts or do you underline a choice phrase
   or two in fiction? A lovely Dickens – sentence or a
   Shakespearean thing. Do you underline?

IAN. Um. Some. Sometimes.

SARAH. What about letters? Do you underline letters?

IAN. Who from?

SARAH. The bank. British Gas. Friends. Family. Lovers.
   Letters from other people. So you can skim-read them and
   not have to…

IAN. No. Not… Well. Some[times] –

SARAH. Yeah? Interesting.

IAN. Um... yeah, just... when things matter – I like to remember them.

SARAH shifts her weight from one foot to the other. She looks at IAN. For some reason she likes this.

SARAH. Do you?

IAN. Yeah.

SARAH. Yeah.

IAN thinks, and then exits again. SARAH looks around, sees the bed and stalks over to it. She looks at it a moment and then suddenly pulls back the duvet. She laughs at herself. She touches the sheets underneath. And then bends and smells the sheets. Then she laughs. Then she calls out.

You don't mind if I check your sheets, do you?

IAN re-enters on the bounce.

IAN. What?

He looks at the bed.

SARAH. I slept with one guy – the other day, I am a bit of a slut, by the way – whose sheets were so greasy, it almost made me sick. They smelt of old sweat and greasy hair and they were horrible to sleep on. Horrible.

I'm not promising anything, just better to know the full facts before making a decision. As the bishop said to the abortionist.

With his thumb up her bottom... Or...

He thinks of how to respond to that, he can't, he exits. He re-enters, carrying a tray of drinks, he puts them down on his coffee table. He smoothes down a cushion and puts it where she might sit on the sofa. Then he sits on the other sofa. He doesn't look at her the entire time. He can't. This whole thing is slightly too real.

IAN. Why don't we...? We could drink these sitting down... Watch the...

He puts on the TV. He looks at what's happening.

She watches him with a smile. He turns and looks at her. He calculates what he's just done.

Sorry.

SARAH. No.

IAN. That was…

He turns off the TV miserably.

SARAH. Not for me. Don't turn off for me. You can have the… It's your party.

They sit in silence. Then he thinks and turns on some music. He's not sure what's in his hi-fi. It's Donna Summer. He turns and looks at her.

IAN. Sorry.

She looks at him for a long time. She's trying to work him out.

SARAH. For which bit?

IAN. Which bit?

SARAH. Do you change them before every Party party – in case you get lucky? Or do you save the bed for best and normally sleep on the floor wrapped in a towel?

IAN. What?

SARAH. The sheets. They're clean, Mr Sheen.

IAN. Oh.Yes. Truth is, my mum's coming round tomorrow – so I cleaned.

SARAH. So this *is* clean, and you were being a little camp about 'It's so messy'. What time's she getting here?

IAN. Oh, don't worry, not 'til lunchtime…

SARAH. So when I do stay over, you mean, I will have ample time to escape before I humiliate you?

IAN. No, no, I didn't mean… I just meant you probably had work. I mean, if you stay. It's when, not… if… I mean… I don't know what I'm saying.

She's looking at him closely now. She smiles.

SARAH. No, okay.

IAN. Sorry. Pathetic is as pathetic does, and…

She smiles. And holds eye contact.

SARAH. Are you pathetic? Number two. Ian.

Oh God, I am drunk, I'm feeling quite emotional. I need to pee.

Other people cry when they get emotional, I just need to pee. Same waterworks, different button, as my mum always used to – no. I can hold it.

Pause. She stands up, downs the pint of water in one easy chug, and starts dancing. In fact, she does a little dance for him. She wants him to join in, but doesn't indicate he should. When he doesn't join in, the dance becomes a little elongated, in a sort of odd way. It lasts for about forty seconds. Then SARAH stands there looking shy.

I don't normally get this drunk.

IAN. Okay.

SARAH. I mean, I'm a slut, granted. But I normally go home with the guy I fancied, not the other guy.

IAN starts to gently laugh. SARAH laughs too.

SARAH. I like that. You're humourful.

IAN. Sorry. I'm just… I don't do this much and this is becoming increasingly – surreal. If you want to leave…

SARAH. 'Surreal'?

Pause. She doesn't leave. Neither say anything for a long time. She does some more hip-swayage/dancing. He looks at his hands. IAN is not good at silence.

IAN. I just – don't know what you're doing here…

Pause.

Did you vote?

SARAH. Are you nice, Ian?

IAN. I'd like to be.

SARAH. How nice?

IAN. Uh, in, um – in what respect?

SARAH. If I was to ask a hundred of your friends – in a very *Family Fortunes*-type way – I was Cilla Black, I am Les Dennis – I am Les Dennis in a very Jeremy-Beadle-type disguise – even given myself tits – I am Les Dennis and we asked a hundred of your friends: 'What do you think of when you think of Ian?' – And your friends – would they say: 'He's nice'?

IAN *considers this and smiles.*

IAN. Yeah. They probably would. Which probably makes me extraordinarily dull.

SARAH. Not really.

People say they hate the word 'nice' because it's meaningless. I actually think it's got a very specific meaning.

It's about a glow, isn't it? Or a –

IAN. Maybe.

Pause. She looks at him even more carefully. He's feeling slightly intimidated.

SARAH. Yes. It's a glow. A glow. A glow in the dark. A Glow-in-the-Dark Batman. Did you have a Glow-in-the-Dark Batman when you were a kid?

IAN. No.

SARAH *stops for a moment, flexes her arm, shifts her weight, and then turns and looks at him again.*

She makes a Family Fortunes *buzzer noise. 'Bi-baa.' She laughs. He sort of laughs. She looks at him, her face has sunk slightly.*

SARAH. Will you be nice to me if I told you some stuff?

IAN. I'm a good listener, if that's what you –

SARAH (*she sings*).
> Cross over the road, my friend,
> Ask the Lord His strength to lend,
> His compassion has no end,
> Cross over the road.

IAN. Stop.

SARAH. Did you have to sing that in school?

IAN. Sarah…

SARAH. I feel like an eleven-year-old girl…

IAN. Sarah…

SARAH. Then again, I feel like an eleven-year-old most of the time.

She approaches, she indicates what she wants, they kiss slowly. He breaks off.

He looks at her a long, long time.

IAN. I think you…

She kisses him again. They break off. She licks her lips. She takes off her top. It's a bit of a struggle, being drunk her arms don't fit through the holes and her head is a struggle and a half.

No… No.

SARAH. Take off your top.

She undoes her bra. He looks at her tits. They scare him. They're not scary tits. But for him…

IAN. I thought you wanted to, uh, talk about something.

SARAH. Enough talking –

She kisses him again. She pulls up his top. He resists, she pulls it off quite aggressively. She slides her hand down his body.

Nipples. I have nipples. Do you like my nipples? I think they look like raspberries two days past their best…

IAN. That's…

SARAH. You wouldn't be taking advantage… Think of it like a punctuation mark. A full stop. Or maybe a semi-colon.

She opens his fly, and puts her hand inside. He tries to stop her. She giggles.

Take it back. A colon.

He pulls his hips back from her.

IAN. Sarah… Stop. Let's talk –

SARAH (*all fire*). NO! You weren't interested in talking.

IAN dislocates. Both are surprised by her outburst.

Sorry. Didn't mean to shout.

She makes the Family Fortunes *buzzer noise again.*

Wrong, Sarah. Wrong.

She kisses him again. This time she misses his mouth.

If you're worried you'll be raping me. I consent.

She picks up his phone. She speaks into it.

I consent.

She puts the phone down.

IAN. Please. I think we should stop.

She does stop. She looks at him.

SARAH. 'We'? No 'we' in it, really, was there?

She wobbles.

Are you a Christian? Most Liberal Democrats I meet are Christians. Not that I meet many Liberal Democrats.

She sways slightly.

IAN. I think you should go home. I don't think you want this –

He looks at her slowly. He picks up his top and starts to put it back on. She stops him with an easy hand. They stand there, semi-naked, in the middle of his room. She seemingly doesn't notice. But she looks oddly vulnerable nonetheless.

SARAH. When I was younger I knew a boy called Ian – and, uh... he was the love of my life. A nice boy, odd like you, he used to walk in front of me when we walked in the park. Why? So he could kill any snakes hiding in the grass.

IAN. I don't take – advantage – of people.

SARAH. He was eleven, so it wasn't an affectation. So it's nothing to be admired...

IAN. It's not about being good – just... it wouldn't be that – fun –

SARAH. And then we met up when he was older and we had sex a few times and actually he was really odd.

He'd only have sex with me in the bath. It was fine, felt a bit sticky at the end but, uh, not too bad.

She turns on Donna Summer again, and turns it right up.

Strangest rim. Got the strangest rim around it. The bath. All sorts of liquids float to the top when you have sex in the bath. Had to scrub it with Clorox. One time – one time he persuaded me to have sex in the bath when I was on my period. Like *Jaws*! Now that was a rim! Doesn't matter. Anyway.

IAN. What's –

SARAH *leans in and whispers in his ear. She continues to do so for up to a minute. The thing she tells him devastates him.*

SARAH. And now we've talked. And now you've listened.

She laughs. Then does a half-hearted attempt at the Family Fortunes *buzzer noise.*

He just stands there.

IAN. On the street –

SARAH. No.

IAN. On the street –

SARAH. No, no. I don't want to talk about it…

IAN. But –

SARAH. No. No. You said you were a good listener. Not a good talker. I don't need a talker.

They sit in silence for a moment, she turns her hand over and looks at it carefully. She looks at her tits. She thinks about covering up her nudity, but changes her mind.

She notices a mark on her skirt and scratches at it.

He tries not to look at her. Then he does look at her, very deliberately.

IAN *gently takes her hand. She looks at his hand. Then she disentangles herself from it, reaches out and takes a glass of wine and slurps.*

What is this fucking music?

IAN. Donna Summer.

SARAH. Right.

IAN walks across and turns it off.

She takes another slurp on her wine.

I just wanted to tell someone – needed to – someone who wasn't – who didn't want to make me a fucking cup of tea and put their fingers on my forehead – I've done so much of that – I told you because you're not a talker, but you seem nice. And you have a very nice bum. And you didn't want to take advantage of me.

IAN. But –

SARAH. Now – (*She puts her hands over his eyes.*) say one about me, one feature about me, and it can't be bum, because I said that, or eyes, mouth, or legs because they're boring.

Or personality.

Definitely not personality.

Or cunt or tits, because –

Or belly button.

I had an ex-boyfriend who said belly button. I liked that as an answer, but then he kept licking it during sex, which is not what I meant at all... And it's put me off belly-button people for life, so don't be one of them.

IAN. You've got nice ears...

SARAH. Okay. Go on...

SARAH takes a moment to herself to show the full anguish of what's happened to her. This isn't big, it's small and controlled, but it's immensely private and the hand over IAN's eyes means it's kept that way.

IAN. What?

SARAH. You have to describe them. You can't have just thought it up. So describe them – just to prove you weren't lying...

IAN. I don't...

SARAH. Big? Small? Do they stick out? To what degree do they stick out?

Pause.

IAN. You're – very brave.

She releases his eyes and kisses him aggressively. He breaks off. She sighs.

You are. You're very – brave.

She looks at him.

SARAH. No, I'm not.

She was my life and now she's not and that's – that's not bravery. That's tragedy.

IAN. My mum's dying, she's – um – she's coming up tomorrow to go see a cancer – I mean, it's just boring cancer.

SARAH. Okay –

IAN. I wasn't saying – it's not the same.

SARAH. No, it's not.

Pause.

IAN. When she told me. My dad left her – I'm sort of the most important person in her life. I wasn't quite sure what to say or do. I wanted to laugh. I'm better at it now, she's coming up to see a specialist. I arranged it.

SARAH. Good for you.

IAN. Did you ever – when my granddad died – I remember going with my dad to the funeral – and we had to sing a hymn. 'We Plough the Fields and Scatter.' Or something like –

SARAH *smiles.*

SARAH. I know it. It's no 'Cross Over the Road'. But it's a hymn.

IAN. Did you know it has two possible tunes that can go with it? My grandma chose it because of one of these tunes, but you don't specify a tune to go with the hymn when choosing hymns and the organist chose to play the other tune. Which no one can sing along with. So this – small crematorium – that I was in – stood there and tried desperately to mumble their way through this hymn that they didn't know… Mostly old people, mumbling their – all consonants and – I started to laugh.

SARAH. It sounds funny.

IAN. But I was standing by my dad – who'd lost his dad – and he was about to give the speech – whatever you call those speeches and I shouldn't have laughed.

Pause.

I'm not very good with death.

SARAH. Is anyone?

IAN. Yeah. Some people are.

Pause.

I'm not very good at many things, really…

SARAH. No.

IAN. I feel like I should – I mean…

She stands and walks towards him.

Shouldn't we… talk… Talking with my mum was…

She stops when she's standing in front of him.

SARAH. Do you want to know the best thing about whispering?

IAN. No.

SARAH. If you do it quiet enough you can't hear what you're saying…

SARAH laughs.

SARAH. Today's the birthday. Anniversary. May first. Mayday. Of the… I wasn't with a friend. Many wanted to be with me. My ex-husband wanted to be with me. But I was walking around the streets, and then I saw this party with the lights on and – you all looked very happy. Why did you look so happy?

IAN. We're forecast to do well, tonight.

SARAH. You're forecast to do well, you looked happy. And so I went inside and here I am… With the wrong man in the wrong flat at the wrong time. But at least next year this'll be the anniversary of something else.

IAN. Yeah. The election or the…

IAN nods.

SARAH. Or you.

IAN. Or me.

They look at each other.

Pause. She picks up her top and pulls it on. She is finally not naked. This is a sort of good thing. It's also a full stop. IAN semi-smiles.

SARAH. Do you want to put the TV on?

Pause.

Go on. Put the telly on…

IAN *hesitates and then sits. And then he turns the telly on. She sits beside him.*

Have you won any yet?

IAN. Yeah.

She turns and looks at him with a gentle smile.

SARAH. But you're not going to win the whole thing? You can't win the whole thing?

IAN *laughs.*

IAN. Oh no… No… definitely not…

SARAH *laughs.*

SARAH. And who's that man?

IAN. That's, um, Portillo. Michael Portillo.

SARAH. Should I know him…?

IAN. No.

SARAH. He doesn't look happy.

IAN. No.

SARAH. Who's the other one?

IAN. I'm not sure.

SARAH. He looks happy.

IAN. Yeah.

Black.

End of Part Two.

PART THREE

7.37 a.m.

A teenage bedroom.

Two boys are sleeping with their arms around each other on a single teenage bed. WILL, *eighteen, self-conscious, gently spooning* JAKE, *eighteen, conscious of self.*

It's gentle. It's kind of beautiful.

JAKE *wakes first, he realises where he is.*

He realises whose arms are around him. He thinks.

He gently dislocates himself.

He sits up on the bed. He's wearing pyjamas. M&S crisp blue pyjamas, the sort of pyjamas that cost a bit.

He rubs his arms.

He exits the room.

WILL *immediately opens his eyes. On the 'B' of the (gentle door) bang. As if he's been waiting for ages. He lies perfectly still. He adjusts his erection.*

He smells his hand.

He looks scared.

He sits up.

He looks more scared.

He's wearing boxer shorts and a T-shirt. He stands and walks around the room, trying to conceal his erection. But it's hard because he's quite a big boy.

He opens a drawer, he looks inside. He picks out a pair of socks. He examines them.

He hears a noise.

He lies down again.

He then shuts his eyes as JAKE *re-enters the room.*

JAKE *has a stack of newspapers. All the tabloids. And an apple. Which is green. He sits cross-legged on the floor. He starts flicking through.*

He stops at a page. He covers it over. He talks in a whisper.

JAKE. Jack Cunningham –

Jack Cunningham –

Jack Cunningham –

Jack Cunningham –

JAKE *stands and begins to strip out of his pyjamas.*

He stops and looks at WILL. *He carries on stripping.*

Jack Jack Jack Jack. Jack in the box.

He picks out a pair of briefs from his chest of drawers.

He puts them on. Delicately, and with a little sorrow as if he enjoyed the nudity.

Then he takes a shirt out of his wardrobe and puts that on.

Cunningham Cunningham –

Richie Cunningham Richie Cunningham –

Jack in the box. Cunningham –

Richie Cunningham in a box. Richie Cunningham in a box. Richie Cunningham in a box. *Happy Days* are dead. Jack Cunningham.

He sits in his pants and shirt and looks at the page.

WILL *opens his eyes and looks at* JAKE.

JAKE *covers the page over.*

WILL *closes his eyes again.*

Alistair Darling Alistair Darling –

Alistair Alistair Alistair –

He does up his shirt buttons and finds a pair of black trousers, he pulls them on.

Then starts putting on his school tie.

He looks at WILL *again.*

He raises his voice slightly.

Darling Darling Darling –

Will you check the stairs, Darling?

I love you, Darling, will you check the stairs?

I love your stairs, Darling.

Darling Darling Darling, Will, are you awake?

WILL *says nothing.*

Will… because you're not making any noise at all, and normally, when people sleep,they make some noise, so are you awake?

Beat.

WILL *opens his eyes, thinks, and then closes them again.*

And then opens them.

WILL. Uh. Yeah.

JAKE. Did I… [wake you]?

WILL. No.

JAKE. How long have you been…?

WILL. I don't…

JAKE. Yeah?

WILL. How long since I made a noise? I mean, it's probably… I should make more… I'll remember that for next time…

JAKE. Yeah.

   Beat.

   Yeah.

WILL. What are you...?

JAKE. Remembering the cabinet. Memorising. Trying to. I
    figured Sharpey might... Sorry, I'd have done it downstairs
    but Mum's asleep on the sofa again and Liz's in the kitchen
    trying to pretend like last night wasn't important and doing
    her nails really loudly. Which smelt. Nail polish. Which isn't
    even a good smell. Though, sort of sends you high,
    according to her.

WILL. Who've you got...?

JAKE. I'm starting with the... You heard about Frank Dobson?

WILL. No.

JAKE. Straight in. Health Secretary. They think.

WILL. Yeah?

JAKE. Yeah.

WILL. Wow.

JAKE. Yeah. Pretty huge.

WILL. I don't even know... where he came from...

JAKE. Select committees, I think. I mean, no... I don't know.
    It's a big promotion...

He looks for and reads.

Environment. He was environment. Shit. I should have...
[known] that. Which is now – I think, Prescott. Part of
Prescott's super ministry, have you? Oh. That's...

JAKE*'s radio alarm suddenly goes off.*

It's 'Things Can Only Get Better' by D:Ream.

JAKE *smiles at* WILL, *does a little dance,* WILL *sort of
copies him. They do a strange unrehearsed semi-
synchronised dance.*

JAKE *starts miming the singing. Then turns it off. Halfway
through a sentence.*

WILL. Wow.

JAKE. Yeah. Yeah.

Beat. WILL *thinks and then sits up.*

WILL. Did we – drink a lot last night?

JAKE. No. Not…

WILL. We didn't.

JAKE. No?

WILL. No.

JAKE. I mean, a bit… toasted a few in. Toasted a few out. Lots of toast. With red jam on top.

WILL *smiles.*

WILL. I thought we…

JAKE. A bit.

WILL. Yeah. Because we didn't top-and-tail and that… In bed, I mean…

JAKE. Yeah. Yeah. I wondered about that too.

WILL. Bladdered – probably –

JAKE. Yeah.

WILL. Frank Dobson.

JAKE. Yeah. For some reason I have no problem remembering his name. Frank Dobson. Dobbing in Frank's son. For some reason that's…

WILL (*laugh*). Dobbing in Frank – I'll remember…

JAKE. Dobbing in Frank's son. Yeah. Yeah. I'm all about the memory – aids –

WILL *counts visibly under his breath – one, two, three – and stands up. He looks down, his erection is no longer visible. He looks up,* JAKE *is looking at him strangely.*

WILL. What?

JAKE. And we played that card game.

WILL. Yeah? Do you think Sharpey will test us?

JAKE. Yeah. I don't know. Maybe... 'Be prepared', though, so... Dib-dib-dib.

WILL. Do you think I should...?

JAKE. I don't know.

Pause. JAKE smiles.

Oh, there's one you'll love – Dad bought me all the papers, left them on the doormat before he –

WILL. Wow. I like the way he...

JAKE. Yeah. He's cool.

He knew I'd want all the papers.

He's on a – he's quite cool with me at the moment because of the whole – you know – but he knew I'd want all the – and he's out of the house at five at the moment – so he must have went to the twenty-four-hour before...

WILL. Yeah. That's really cool.

JAKE. Anyway, one you'll like – the *Star*'s all – 'It's a new Dawn – um, actually her name is Gaynor.'

He searches through the stack and finds a copy of the Star. *It's got a picture of a topless model on the front (she's Gaynor). WILL laughs.*

WILL. Oh, that's really [funny] –

JAKE. Isn't it?

WILL. She's properly...

JAKE. I know.

WILL. Not really my [type] –

JAKE. No. Nor me. A bit...

WILL. Big.

JAKE. Yeah.

They both look at the picture again. Slightly scared.

Yeah. Big. Yeah. Well.

WILL. What did the *Guardian* say?

JAKE. Oh. He didn't buy that one, just the tabloids.

WILL. Right.

JAKE. I think he thought I'd just want the [tabloids], plus –
    they are a bit cheaper than the...

WILL. Yeah. Still. My dad would never...

JAKE. Your dad's great. I love talking to your dad.

WILL. Yeah. He's...

JAKE. No. Seriously. He's great. He's brilliant. He can fix
    things. My dad can literally fix nothing.

WILL. Yeah, that's – nothing's broken in my house.

JAKE. Well, nothing's broken in this house either. My dad just
    gets someone in.

WILL. Yeah.

    JAKE laughs.

JAKE. I mean, who do you think irons my shirts? Mum?

WILL. Yeah.

JAKE. I mean... there's plenty that lady probably thinks she
    can do – but she can't – and even if she could – ironing shirts
    – not top of the list.

    JAKE laughs. WILL looks at him.

WILL. Yeah.

    *JAKE gets some scissors and then sits on the floor and starts
    cutting out articles for his scrapbook.*

JAKE. He left a note on the papers – 'Were you still up for
    Portillo?' Which I thought was quite –

WILL. Yeah.

JAKE. He probably heard it on the radio but still…

WILL. We were.

JAKE. Yeah.

WILL. We were still up for Rifkind, actually. Was that before or…?

JAKE. I can't remember.

WILL. We probably were still up when your dad got up to… I mean, we can't have got more than two hours… three hours…

JAKE. Yeah. I don't know when…

WILL. I don't feel tired.

JAKE. No?

WILL. No. Probably adrenalin. Or nail-polish fumes that have – transcended the [floors] –

JAKE. I bet Sharpey will make us do loads of stuff.

WILL. Maybe.

JAKE. I bet he'll…

WILL. Maybe. Still, I'm not tired so…

JAKE. No. I'm not saying I am. I'm not tired. I can always tell when I'm tired and hiding it from myself. I start to sing songs.

WILL. Great.

JAKE. And I'm not singing songs. Well, other than – do you think Carla will be in…?

WILL. Maybe.

JAKE. I bet she will. I'll bet she'll be done – all the – she'll know all the Cabinet off by…

WILL. Yeah. Probably. And then she'll give you that look she gives you when she gets stuff better than you.

JAKE. Yeah. Maybe.

WILL. Ever since you fingered her by the swings after the *Westminster Live* thing.

JAKE. Oh. Yeah.

WILL. Ever since you got into Cambridge and she [didn't] –

JAKE. Yeah. More that than…

WILL. Yeah.

JAKE. The finger. Ing. Though, I think if she'd applied for SPS rather than Law she'd have… definitely not got…

WILL. No. She's not as clever as you.

JAKE. She is. Carla. Definitely.

WILL. She isn't.

JAKE *waves the scissors in the air.*

JAKE. She is. She got far better GCSEs…

WILL. What do they…? Anyway, you weren't even really trying then…

JAKE. Yeah.

WILL. She isn't.

JAKE. She is.

WILL. She isn't. It's what I like about you, you don't know how good you are. Clever. Good.

JAKE. Okay.

WILL. Not to…

JAKE. You've gone [red] –

WILL. No.

JAKE *giggles, enjoying this.*

JAKE. Yeah, your cheeks are all… crimson. Silken crimson. Silken crimssssson.

WILL. Not really.

JAKE. I don't really fancy her any more anyway…

WILL. Carla?

JAKE. I mean, I never really did. I only – because she basically offered.

WILL. We were all quite drunk.

JAKE. Yeah. And then the fingering just sort of – I mean, she basically put my hand in her… knickers and – you know – I felt like – I mean, it was – I didn't even touch her tits, which was [odd]. Well, only through clothing. How does that – ? Twat touch but no nipple touch, that's a strange girl.

WILL. Yeah.

JAKE. Anyway, you got up to something that night, didn't you, with, uh…? With –

WILL. No.

JAKE. Not Tessa or Emma or someone…

WILL. No.

JAKE. I think Emma fancies you.

WILL. Does she?

JAKE. She told me the other day that you had really cute freckles.

WILL. Really cute [freckles]?

JAKE. Yeah. On your face.

WILL. Okay.

JAKE (*replicating Shaggy's 'Mr Boombastic'*). 'Mr Luvva Luvva.' She's not wrong…

WILL. What?

> JAKE *suddenly gets* WILL *in a headlock.*

What? No. Get off.

> JAKE *sort of tries to do a sort of judo knuckle-crunch on the top of* WILL*'s head, and then he laughs and dislocates.*

JAKE. God.

WILL. Yeah.

> WILL *gingerly fingers his head.* JAKE *looks at him and laughs. And then smiles. And then frowns.*

JAKE. Emma.

WILL. Yeah.

JAKE. Emma.

WILL. Yeah.

JAKE. She's got a nice bum.

WILL. Has she?

JAKE. Yeah. And she's clever without being too clever. She's just the right sort of clever, I think. For a girlfriend.

WILL. Yeah?

JAKE. Yeah. Will you ask her out, then?

WILL. No. Not really my [type]. You could have fucked her. Carla. You could have...

JAKE. No...

WILL. You could.

JAKE. Not without build-up. And build-up's dull... Besides, I don't really have time at the moment anyway. For the dull build-up.

WILL. Yeah.

JAKE. Yeah. And twat not nipple is just...

> *Pause. The two boys look at each other. And then look away.*

Funny word... 'fucked'.

WILL. Yeah. I hate using it.

JAKE. So... big.

WILL. Yeah. Big.

JAKE. It's the 'F' – it's a brutal-sounding consonant. But sex sounds so…

WILL. Yeah. And making love! I mean!

JAKE. Shagging?

WILL. Bonking?

JAKE. Rutting?

WILL. Skootching.

JAKE. Mooching.

WILL. Banging.

JAKE. Donkey-Konging.

WILL. Hmmm-and-haaaing.

JAKE. Doing the do-se-do.

WILL. Meating – M-E-A-T-ing.

JAKE. Yeah.

WILL. Yeah.

JAKE. Yeah.

WILL. Shagging's probably better… best.

JAKE (*Churchill impression*). 'Democracy is the worst form of government apart from all the others…' You know. Churchill.

WILL (*laughs, sort of*). Yeah.

Beat.

JAKE. Aren't you going to get ready?

WILL. What?

JAKE. Changed. For school. I won't look.

WILL. Okay.

Pause. JAKE thinks and then sets his chair from the desk so it's facing towards the audience. He sits in it. He faces front.

He knows exactly what he's doing. He's got a prickish look in his eyes.

JAKE. You're going to have such a great time in Leeds.

WILL. Yeah?

WILL isn't sure what he should be doing. So he's doing nothing.

JAKE. I really wanted to do that course.

WILL. Well, it's your reserve, though, so…

WILL stands. He takes off his T-shirt.

He folds his arms over his chest.

He watches JAKE so-so-so carefully.

JAKE. Yeah.

WILL. If you don't get the grades…

JAKE. Yeah. But don't make it like that…

WILL. No. I –

JAKE. Because it's not. It's just, Cambridge is Cambridge, right? I mean, it just is…

WILL. Part of me hopes you don't get the grades.

JAKE. No.

WILL. Though, if you didn't, I probably wouldn't either, and then you'd be going to Leeds and I'll go to Middlesex and…

JAKE. No. You'll get your…

WILL. You'll definitely get yours.

JAKE. I don't know.

WILL. No. You will.

JAKE. Do you really think so?

WILL. Definitely.

JAKE. I hope so. I mean, I'm working hard enough, so…

WILL. Definitely.

JAKE. Still, three As…

WILL. I know.

JAKE. With my GCSEs –

WILL. Yeah, but you didn't try in GCSE –

JAKE. Yeah. I know.

WILL. Whereas, this time…

JAKE. I read a textbook the other weekend. The whole thing.

WILL. Yeah?

JAKE. You really think I will…? You wouldn't…?

WILL. Definitely.

WILL thinks and then turns around and pulls off his boxer shorts.

He then realises he hasn't got his new boxer shorts ready and looks for his bag.

He sees it.

Beside JAKE's chair.

He thinks about pulling up his boxer shorts again, but dismisses the thought; he cups his bollocks in his hand, and then turns and looks at JAKE. He is still facing forward.

WILL thinks and then lets go of the cup and bravely walks up and picks up his bag as if it's nothing.

The boys brush against each other.

Both stiffen. WILL slightly more openly.

JAKE. Well, whatever…

WILL. You will. And then you'll be Prime Minister. Probably the youngest ever.

JAKE. Blair's forty-three.

WILL starts to pull on his clothes rapidly.

WILL. You'll be…

JAKE. Youngest since Lord Liverpool, who was forty-two
    when he became Prime Minister in 1812.

WILL. You can do that.

JAKE. Who was the youngest since… William Pitt was twenty-
    four, when he became – in 1783 –

WILL. Well, maybe not [that] –

> JAKE *starts to laugh,* WILL *laughs too. Neither quite know
> why.*

> I think you could beat Blair. I mean, that's twenty-five years,
> and think all the stuff you've achieved by the time you're
> eighteen.

JAKE. And what will you…?

WILL. I'll be your Chancellor or something…

JAKE. No. You'd need Economics and Maths for that…

WILL. Really? I'm shit at…

JAKE. Yeah. The Civil Servants will walk all over you if you
    haven't – it's why I wish I did A-level Maths.

WILL. You did Economics.

JAKE. Yes, but Maths…

WILL (*considering*). Maybe you should have done it instead of
    History?

JAKE. You could be Chief Whip. Thy will be done.

WILL. Yeah?

JAKE. It's a surprisingly… surprisingly influential position.

WILL. Yeah.

JAKE. Other than the big four it's probably the position works
    closest with the Prime Minister.

WILL. Yeah? Yeah.

JAKE. God. Sorry. Why am I talking like you know nothing about politics? Sorry. Sorry.

WILL. No. I –

JAKE. You know loads about politics. You probably know more than me…

WILL. No.

JAKE. No?

WILL. No.

> JAKE *sits back on the floor and resumes cutting out articles.* WILL *watches him.*

> Do you read all of them?

JAKE. They're reference mostly. You don't need to read reference. You just need to have it.

WILL. Right.

JAKE. I put them in a huge file and then when something comes up I have them there. For reference. It's like a dictionary of newspaper clippings.

WILL. Great.

JAKE. I forget you haven't been in my room much.

WILL. Not much. We generally just –

JAKE. You know, I'd quite like it if we both ended up at the same [place] –

WILL. Yeah?

JAKE. University.

WILL. Yeah?

JAKE. We could do the first year in halls…

WILL. What [halls]?

JAKE. Student accommodation. Basically it means these huge blocks built by the –

WILL. Oh, I've seen those. Yeah. Halls of residence. I get what you're... Just call them... abbreviate them to 'halls', do they? I don't know much about – accommodation...

JAKE. That's because neither of your parents went to university.

WILL. Yeah. Probably. I mean, I know some stuff...

JAKE. First year in halls, and then we could get a flat or something in our second year.

WILL. Okay. Yeah. That sounds [great].

JAKE. I mean, it's not a problem, your parents having not gone to university.

WILL. No. I know.

JAKE. You're exactly what the Party is all about, frankly. You're the reason I'm pleased Dad couldn't afford to send me to private school.

WILL. Yeah.

JAKE. And sometimes we could go out into Leeds and try and pull or whatever and sometimes we could stay in. And you know, that year abroad thing could be...

WILL. In America.

JAKE. Exactly. Maybe I should reject Cambridge if I get in...

WILL. Yeah?

JAKE. No. Probably –

WILL. No.

Pause.

JAKE. We just got to concentrate on getting that second term – I mean, with this mandate – but still... it could...

WILL. Yeah.

JAKE. But if we concentrate, if we keep moving forward, if we stick to our promises, we could –

WILL. Yeah.

JAKE *moves and wants to clap his hands, but doesn't.*

JAKE. Anyway. Do you want brekkie-breakfast?

WILL. Do you?

JAKE. Liz might be out of the kitchen by now. Depending on whether she thinks it's important to wash before [school] or just do her nails. Is it weird washing after you do your – ?

WILL. I'm not going to [wash] –

JAKE. No time. But breakfast – Dad keeps a good range of cereal in.

WILL. Okay.

JAKE. None of those party packs or… Full-size boxes. Just – a few of them, rather than one. Me and Dad eat plenty of cereal.

WILL. Okay.

JAKE. And I like a range. I like a range of cereal. And there's never enough in a fun-size.

WILL. No. I know what you mean…

JAKE. And we could memorise the new Cabinet together.

WILL. Yeah. Who's Chief Whip?

JAKE. Exactly! I have no idea. It'd be brilliant if both of us knew everything.

WILL. I know.

JAKE. Not just to show Carla or anything…

WILL. I know.

JAKE. I'm never fingering her again anyway, so…

WILL. Yeah…? Yeah.

JAKE. She had too much pubic hair too.

WILL. Yeah?

JAKE. Yeah, I couldn't tell if I was hitting… if I was hitting the right [places] –

WILL. Yeah?

JAKE. I did. But it took me a while.

WILL. Yeah.

JAKE makes for the door.

And then stops.

He turns with a tumescent smile.

JAKE. Will…

WILL. Yeah.

JAKE. Can you believe it?

WILL. No.

JAKE. We crushed them.

WILL. I know. And I like how it's 'we' too.

JAKE. Of course it's… We leafleted Slough, Ascot and Reading West. Martin Salter. We canvassed where they let us. It's definitely… It's 'we'. It's 'us'.

WILL. Yeah.

JAKE. I'm really… I can't believe how good I feel.

WILL. I know.

JAKE. I feel powerful.

WILL. You are. We are.

JAKE. Like He-Man. 'I – have – the – power.'

WILL (*giggles*). I'll be Man-At-Arms.

JAKE. She-Ra, right right. She-Ra, right.

WILL. The tiger thing. What was the tiger – called?

JAKE. I don't know. I've never watched much kids' TV.

WILL. No.

JAKE. Seven Cabinet Ministers gone. Half their fucking seats. 418 seats.

WILL. It's amazing.

JAKE. I feel like I can do anything.

WILL. You can. You will. I mean, definitely.

JAKE thinks and then moves to hug WILL. They hesitate a moment and then they hug. JAKE's back is towards us, but we see WILL's face really clearly. He's concentrating really hard on not getting an erection.

Then he smells JAKE's hair and can't help himself.

JAKE *dislocates.*

He looks at WILL for a moment. And then JAKE kisses WILL on the mouth. Just a peck but a significant one at that. They hold for a moment.

As he breaks off, JAKE smiles like he's done WILL a huge favour. And WILL smiles because, well…

JAKE. I knew it was going to happen, but not like this…

WILL *tries to digest what just happened.*

WILL. No.

He smiles. And then he doesn't. JAKE is watching him so-so carefully, but he's not showing it. WILL knows everything.

JAKE. Such a majority. Such a…

WILL. Yeah. Jake –

JAKE. It's brilliant. It's like everything's new. I'm so excited.

WILL. Yeah? Jake –

JAKE. What?

WILL *takes a sniff and then a breath.*

He opens his mouth to speak. JAKE turns to look at him.

Spit it out.

WILL *says nothing*. JAKE *laughs*.

As the bishop said to the choirboy.

WILL. I – um – come to – come to Leeds with me –

JAKE. What?

WILL *thinks how to say it differently; he can't.*

WILL. Come to Leeds.

JAKE *looks at* WILL *closely*. WILL *swallows*.

JAKE. I can't. I'd be – betraying – myself.

WILL. Okay. Okay.

Beat. WILL *nods. Then nods again*. JAKE *just keeps looking at him.*

Remember I asked, though, won't you?

JAKE *turns away – he knows what* WILL *means.*

JAKE. Yeah. Of course.

Beat.

And maybe I won't get the grades so…

WILL. Okay.

JAKE. No. No. I'm pleased you've asked. I could make sure you'd stay good. You'd – (*Like ET.*) be good.

He touches WILL*'s nose. And then his heart.*

(*Like ET.*) Be good. You are good.

Then he smiles.

You're – good.

The two boys stare at each other for a moment more.

JAKE *breaks first, with a grin.*

My dad told me once there was two clues to getting along in life: never go to a supermarket when you're hungry and never make a decision when you've got an erection. He was drunk. Which I guess is probably another clue – never give your child advice when drunk. I think there's one clue really – enjoy what you've got when you get it and then try and keep it.

We're going to be great.

Mark the moment.

JAKE *grins and exits.* WILL *hesitates a moment, looks around the room and smiles. And then doesn't smile.*

WILL. Yeah.

WILL *exits.*

Slow fade. Black.

The End.

BUNNY

For Teresa Topolski

with illustrations by
Jenny Turner

Bunny was first produced by nabokov and Escalator East to Edinburgh in association with Watford Palace Theatre and Mercury Theatre, Colchester, at Underbelly Cowgate at the Edinburgh Festival Fringe, on 5 August 2010, performed by Rosie Wyatt.

Director	Joe Murphy
Designer	Hannah Clark
Illustrations	Jenny Turner
Video Designer	Ian William Galloway
Lighting Designer	Rick Mountjoy

KATIE, *eighteen*

Okay, it's hot.

And I'm late leaving school because of orchestra practice.

And Abe. Sort of my boyfriend, sort of my not, is sitting waiting on the wall by the school gate. Because, you know, we don't get much time together and so walking home is sort of a thing with us.

'Alright,' he says, without smiling. On the wall. Shoulders hunched.

'Alright.'

I play clarinet. Not well. But I'm carrying my clarinet case – because of orchestra practice – and my bag. Abe is not carrying anything because he's not at the school. He's a bit older. Twenty-four. He works in the offices at Vauxhall. 8 'til 4 so that works, fits, with my school day. He's good-looking. Well. He's also black.

Not that that – I just never know how to bring that up.

I didn't bring that up with my parents for ages – until he came round and I could see they were surprised. And then later I heard them talking in the kitchen and they said – Mum said 'I knew Abe was a funny name, I told you there'd be something about him'. Not that they're – they read the *Guardian*. And we live next door to some Iranians and they come round all the time. Or they could. The Harandis.

Anyway, we're walking. Hand in hand. Which is okay but I've got my shoulder bag on and my clarinet, so I'm having to have them both on the right-hand side while holding hands with him on the left. And they're sort of too big and banging against my hip as we walk. Not that I have hips.

Sometimes we have quite a bit to say to each other. He's not much of a talker, but he can talk. But today it's hot – and I think he's had quite a hard day, so that's... He doesn't like his job. Because of the people he works with mainly. He works in the office. He likes the people who work in the factory down below, but office people just aren't his people.

He told me once my parents were sort of like the people who work in the office, but I'm more factory... It was a compliment.

Anyway, I'm sort of talking – for us both – about the spots between my shoulder blades because I'm classy and about my A levels because – and about orchestra because I've just been in orchestra and it's sometimes quite funny – and I'm jabbering but that's okay because Abe's pretty zoned-out.

'You want an ice cream?' He says. Interrupting a particularly interesting thing about how someone put a tampon up Suzy Brinstead's flute. For jokes. When we did this thing in Bedford.

'What?'

'You want an ice cream? I really need to up my sugar or something, you want an ice cream?' He means blood sugar and he knows he does, but he'd never use a phrase like blood sugar because it sounds too posh. We're walking past the newsagent. He's had a thought.

'No. I'm not doing sweets at the moment.' I say, smiling, while the whiteheads on my back nod in agreement.

'You'll have a bite of mine though?' He says. Hopefully. Or... And I nod and just like that he dislocates from my hand and disappears inside the shop.

And I think and then follow him in.

I always like shops. I like the feeling of everything being available. For a price. I think if I owned a shop, I'd just spend ages staring at all my stuff. I went through a stage, about three years ago, four years ago, of shoplifting – and the trouble was I never shoplifted anything I used – I shoplifted cleaning equipment and things like that.

I kept it.

I didn't use it.

So when my dad caught me I still had everything stacked neatly inside my cupboard – tins of Pledge and posh Brillo Pads – and we went round to every place and gave them their stuff back – I remembered which store each was from which is – psycho – and Dad asked in every place if they wanted to press charges.

None of them did.

Anyway, I just linger as Abe – he roots through this freezer cabinet for his ice creams – he takes ages to make up his mind – and I'm all – as I linger – well, I could nick them J-cloths and no one would notice. My whole life's a hazard. And this kid – Duncan – who I know from school – is stacking boxes in the back. So I go over to him to take my mind off the J-cloths and say 'Alright' – but he doesn't say nothing back and I'm trying to think if I did anything to him and think maybe he was one of those I puked on at the school disco at Christmas. Long story. So I leave that. And then I leave the shop partly to get away from the J-cloths and partly to let Duncan know he hasn't phased me and partly to let Abe know he needs to make up his mind about which flavour Cornetto he wants. Because I won't wait for ever. Though I will probably. And he waited for me outside school – so…

Pause.

We've been together six months, well, five-and-a-half and having sex for the last four months.

He was my first. Which makes me later than most I know.

I'd blown quite a few. More than a few actually. I blew so many that I almost got the nickname of Balloon Girl. Someone tried to start it. Didn't hold. Which is good. For some reason I am the sort of person people have nicknames for. My nickname for ages was Fish. Because – well, I don't even know why my nickname was Fish… But one time, at a parents' evening, I'm with my mum – and Jade, a friend, sort of a friend, a 'friend' you know – shouts across 'Fish, you alright?' And I'm all 'Yeah'. And my mum was sniffing all the car journey home and sat me down that night and asked me whether I had a yeast infection. I think I ended up telling her I was called it because I liked swimming.

No. Lots of blowjobs. Vaginal sex saved for best. Or… something…

He's not particularly big. So that's a myth.

He comes out of the shop and we start walking again. He's got an ice cream so we don't hold hands. Though why you need two hands to hold an ice cream and not two hands to hold a clarinet and a shoulder bag and – you know… Well…

He doesn't say anything. And I'm not babbling so much. So it is more – then, bang –

We'd not walked five metres, him licking, me not talking – which I wish is the story of my life but it isn't – and a kid on a bike comes past and knocks his ice cream out of his hand. And Abe in the confusion of the moment – kicks out in anger at the loss of the ice cream and in the kick – kicks the kid's wheels and sends him sprawling onto the road.

We go from nought to sixty without me even noticing. Ice cream on the floor. Kick. Kid on the floor. Abe standing looking at his dead ice cream.

It's the kid – still laying on the street – that speaks first. 'Fuck d'you do that for?'

And it's his tone or something. But this riles Abe – who says 'My fucking ice cream, you knocked my fucking ice cream.'

'So you kicked me off my bike, you fuck?'

'No. No. I lost my balance.'

The kid. Well, I say kid, he's a man. Just a young one. My age. Maybe. Unruly hair. Slight moustache. Dressed like a Tintin fan. He's scrawny, but well defined, you know? The sort of kid who's been doing press-ups since he was fifteen in the hope of getting a girlfriend but with the sense he never will. He picks up his bike and walks over towards us.

'You kicked me off my bike. Into middle of road. You fuck.'

He's Northern. He's one of those Northern Asians. Not Northern Asian. As in from Northern Asia. Where's Northern Asia? Asia's Asia, right? No. Just Bradford or whatever. Again. I don't know how to bring up the whole race thing... It's a conundrum, that one.

'You knocked off my ice cream. I was enjoying it. I can't eat it now.' Abe says. Fronting up.

Because you don't run away from a fight if you want to work in the factory not the office.

'Listen.' The kid says. Putting his bike down on the floor. I mean, he's not flexing, but he might as well be. 'You just need to say sorry.'

'Fuck off.' Says Abe.

And so the kid spits at him.

Spits.

At Abe. I mean, spit. And it's a lumpy gobby sort of spit. And so Abe slaps him. And then the kid hits him.

And just like that – in front of me – they're fighting.

Now. I don't know much about fighting but I guess the truth about fighting – and I've seen a bit – is that unless it's done well – and it's rarely done well – it looks really shit. Mostly it's hair pulling and grabbing and grappling and little-boy punches you can barely see. I'm not sure I've ever seen a good punch thrown. You know, one that makes a guy spit a tooth out and a gob of blood... You know...

Abe and the kid firstly are fighting standing up, pushed up against the wall like a couple of young lovers desperate to make babies but not sure how. Then one of them – I think it's Abe – but I'm not watching close enough – pushes the kid down on the ground and they have a tumble down there, which includes a dirty bit where Abe grabs the kid's bollocks and twists. And by now a few people are standing and staring but more because the fight is blocking the pavement than... I once saw a monkey pissing in its own mouth at Whipsnade Zoo, and honestly it was way more masculine. This is a pointless fight.

And then just like that – after two minutes max – it's over – the kid has his arm across Abe's throat and he's choking Abe – really choking him and he looks at Abe once and then twice and then Abe nods his head and the kid rolls off and away.

And they both lie there. And then the kid gets up – slightly wobbly – picks up his bike – coughs – repeatedly – cough cough – spits – nowhere near Abe this time – feels his bollocks – checking they're still there – there's one, there's the second – winces and starts rolling down the street.

Like a cowboy that has just done the right thing.

And I know better than to help Abe up. But I know up is where he wants to be.

So I pop a chewing gum in my mouth from my bag because I'm sure my mouth's too dry and my breath's gone to sick. And I hate bad breath. Particularly mine. But I don't brush my teeth enough. True story.

Abe gets up himself after a few goes. He looks at me like he's expecting me to say something. And the truth is, all this has come out of the blue a bit for me. So I've got nothing.

Pause.

There's something about fat people eating, isn't there? I mean, to be honest, I really quite envy what and how they do it. They look like they don't just want to eat the cake, they want to eat their fingers for having the temerity – good word, Abe wouldn't like it – to touch something as nice as the cake. They're sort of – rabid – you know? I mean, I can tell you totally honestly, that I'm pretty sure there's nothing that I care about so much as a fat person cares about cake.

I used to have a fat friend. Sheridan. Named after a Sheffield Wednesday footballer – and they wondered why she ate? Bulimia in the end. She got hospitalised once she turned yellow. Then they moved her from the school – when she got out – of hospital – because they wanted to 'change her routine' and they weren't sure our school was a 'healthy environment'. Like any school is a healthy environment. But I did like watching her eat. With every mouthful you just saw this look of pure gratitude crossing her face – like – I can't believe I'm getting to eat this… this is awesome.

I say 'friend'. She wasn't really. My friends are different. I'm – difficult to explain without sounding thick – but me and her don't fit like that. Not that I fit anywhere. I'm the unfit fitter. I don't fit. But not in a bad way. Just in a – way. To give an instance – and this is true – and very very illustrative – everyone came to my eighteenth-birthday party – I mean, every single one of the twenty-five I invited – and all were important – but also everyone left my birthday party – every single one of the twenty-five – at 10.30 p.m.

Which is not a normal time to leave any birthday party, I know. And that's what I mean about…

But they were bored and it was quite shit and they thought it'd be quite funny to leave, and it sort of was, you know? Funny. Still quite an embarrassing one to explain to your parents. Where are all your friends? Um. Hiding. No. They've gone. Obviously. Where have they gone? Um. Home. Probably. Why? Why have they gone? Turn. Look parents in the eye. Because this was pointless. I basically turned it all on them. Which was fair enough. They'd made some effort. But the wrong effort. And so had I. I mean, it was mostly my fault. There was booze – but there were too many snacks and not enough Ann Summers' toys or something. I don't know.

Anyway, it's not as bad as it sounds…

Still. Mum apologised a week later for it being crap. But she didn't do it well enough. So I stole her wallet. She spent ages looking for it. 'I know I must have left it somewhere.' Turned the house upside down. Had to cancel all her cards. And being

Mum and slightly overcautious about most things, cancelling all
her cards included cancelling her library card – 'I just don't
want to accrue unnecessary fines, that's all.' She said.

I put it in her sock drawer two days later. Minus one pound fifty
exactly just to see if she'd notice. She didn't. She was pleased.
To get it back.

Anyway, that's… what's complicated. That's part of my
resettlement software.

Abe didn't come to the party. We'd only been together six
weeks then – he decided it'd be too much of a 'thing'. That's
when we had sex actually. That night. After he decided he
couldn't come to my birthday party because it was too much of
a commitment I decided that I'd give him my Virginia County.
And I'm clever. I got two As, six Bs at GCSE and I got A, B, B
and C in my AS levels. Ass levels. It's what we…

Pause.

The post-fight atmos is not what it could be. Abe's mood has not improved. He doesn't say nothing – I ask him whether he's okay – he says 'Why wouldn't I be?' And I ask whether his eye hurts and he says to stop asking stupid – fucking questions.

And I don't really notice the car pulling up. And nor does he.

'Abe,' we hear this voice say.

We both turn and look and this sporty-but-shitty-red-short-car-thing. I don't know much about cars. But this is the sort of car that really really wants go-faster stripes down the side. There are two – well, men – inside – one a big guy, the talker – Asian – and one smaller and white.

'Asif.' Abe says, breaking into his first smile of the day. 'Hey man.' And walks across to the car and slaps hands with the big guy.

'You okay, fella?' Asif asks. He's got a tat down his forearm of something in a foreign language – could be his own language but probably isn't – if I had a tattoo I'd have it in tiny writing and it'd say 'will lick for money' – just there on my wrists. Or 'I love Colin' and people will say 'Who's Colin?' And I'd say 'Exactly'.

'Yeah,' says Abe, cocking him a you-think-this-is-hurt-you-should-see-me-when-I've-been-cage-fighting-I'm-not-a-pussy-I-really-really-promise-you-not-a-pussy look. And I've worked out – straight away – because I'm clever with all my GCSEs and Ass-levels like – that Asif – Asif works in the factory. At Vauxhall. Schwing.

'We saw what that prick did to you. Didn't we, Jake?' Asif insists.

And Jake, sitting on the other side of the car raises his eyebrows and says 'Yeah. Prick.' Jake wears the look of a man who has inhaled too much paintstripper.

'What? No.' Says Abe. Flushing now. And I can hear his breathing getting faster. This Asif – he matters. 'No. I got him good as he got me.'

'Did you fuck,' says Asif – lighting a cigarette nonchalantly and having a quick squizz at my tits as he does. And I'm flattered to be honest with you. They aren't much to look at so I'm flattered. Even with padding. 'Get in. We'll find him. We'll sort him out.'

What?

Asif looks at us both. 'Beast won't bite. We can chase him down.'

What?

'Come on. He'll get away.'

And Abe looks at me – uh – and then gets inside the car. And I think…

What?

…And then…

The car smells of cum and weed.

Which is quite a good combination.

And I am inside it with an Asian guy, a black guy and a white guy.

Which is quite a good combination. And also the start of a joke I won't tell.

And I'm –

I'm – excited – I think.

Abe sits on the left behind J-j-j-Jake. I've decided he's a stutterer. He looks like a stutterer and a bed-wetter. I sit behind Asif, right in view of the rear-view mirror.

Once he adjusts it.

So he can look at my tits some more.

And we're set.

And we're go.

And that's good enough for me.

Excitement. Fear. Feariment. Asif guns the accelerator like he's…

We drive fast.

We're chasing a kid – we have to drive fast.

'Who's the lucky lady, Abraham?' Asif asks – looking at me as he swings the car round a particularly tight corner.

'Katie. She's called Katie.' Abe says. And I nod and push out my chest slightly. Just…

And Asif nods and looks at me appreciatively. As he ramps up to fifth gear on a thirty-mile-an-hour stretch of road. We're not going thirty.

I think Asif may have learnt to drive on the dodgems.

'What's in the box?' He asks. He's barely looking at the road.

I look at my clarinet. 'My clarinet.' I say. He nods. I'm not sure he knows what a clarinet is.

And we turn this way and that – scouting the roads for a kid with a head wound on a pushbike. To start with – of course – the kid doesn't know he's being chased. But then we spot him and Asif aims the car straight at him and accelerates. Which is not the most subtle catchy-catchy-monkey tactics I've ever seen. But it lets the kid know what's going on.

And the chase is on.

Now Luton – if you're not aware of this – is a mess of paths and roads. There are loads and loads of paths that lead places between the houses. When I was younger my mum used to walk me everywhere and we'd always take the paths because she liked them. And then when I was ten or so we stopped taking the paths because they scared her. True story.

Anyway, the paths make chasing difficult. We catch a glimpse of him there, he helter-skelters down a path a car can't follow him down, we catch a glimpse of him there, he U-turns, pedals like crazy and disappears again down a rabbit hole.

But Asif, Asif is determined, every time we see him disappear down a path, Abe's like 'Let me out, I'll chase him down, Asif' but Asif is like 'No, bro, no way, no, you're on foot, he's on bike, you'll never catch him, besides, I know these roads like the back of my ex-missus's arse' – he tips me a look – 'I know where that path comes out' and every time he does. Every time he cuts the kid off, and every time the kid just escapes.

Then – we corner him in a cul-de-sac.

Which I think should be the title for a song: 'Cornering You in a Cul-de-Sac'. A love song about anal sex.

And he looks – the kid looks – about and there's nowhere for him to escape to – like a bunny trapped in a fox's eye – and Asif gets out of the car. And Abe thinks and then follows him out. And Jake looks at me, and I get out and he follows.

'Alright' Asif says. To the kid.

The kid says nothing.

'Alright' Asif says again.

We spread across the bottom of this cul-de-sac. We do it without being told to.

'He started on me. He kicked my back wheel.' The kid says, his northern voice wobbling.

'I know.' Asif says looking at Abe. 'What a dick, right?'

And Jake laughs, 'Yeah, a dick' he says.

And Abe looks at Jake and then laughs too.

Then a voice comes from behind us – 'Iqqy, you okay?' And I turn and look. It's a ten-year-old kid sucking on a sherbet sweet.

And Iqqy – that's his name – uses this distraction and takes off at speed. He aims at me. He aims at fucking me, on his bike, and I turn just to see him as he mows past me and I try and kick his bike – but he gets past and then he's riding free.

He makes this cry as he exits the cul-de-sac as we're scrambling back towards the car. This sort of war cry – this –

A-la-la-la la-la.

Sort of Red Indian war cry.

A-la-la-la-la-la.

And then he's gone.

We're all back in the car and seated – sprinting into position – before Asif… But Asif isn't getting in. He's standing over the ten-year-old.

'What's his name?' He asks the ten-year-old.

'What's his name? Where does he live?'

The ten-year-old looks up at Asif and sees he means business.

'What's he done to you? He's okay you know.' The ten-year-old says with – something.

'What's his name?' Asif says again, his tongue working hard to make the words clear. 'Where does he live?'

The ten-year-old sighs like he's forty years older. He wipes his sweaty forehead. I'm melting myself.

'I think I said already.' This ten-year-old is brave. 'He's called Iqqy, I dunno nothing else.'

Asif looks at him and then reaches his hand inside the ten-year-old's trouser pockets and pulls out whatever's inside. He gets a handful of change, a house key and a library card. He probably touches the ten-year-old's dick too.

The ten-year-old doesn't like this. 'No. Don't nick my stuff. Give it back.'

Abe makes to get out of the car. I don't know what he wants to do. He's beginning to annoy me. It's too hot in the car.

Asif smiles at the ten-year-old. 'You going to the library?' He looks at the library card and spies a name. 'Arsched, you going to the library?' The ten-year-old – Arsched – has tears in his eyes now. J-j-j-Jake laughs from inside the car. Abe doesn't. I don't either.

'Please. Give it back.'

Asif gets softer now. 'I ain't gonna hurt you, right, Arsched? Just tell me his name. I know he's Iqqy, what's his full name?'

The ten-year-old thinks, wipes his nose with his hand and shifts his leg from one side to the other like he needs a piss. 'He's called Iqbal Servat. He lives – I don't – somewhere round Marsh Farm.'

Asif looks at him – then nods. 'I believe you.' He says. And he gives Arsched back his library card, his change and his house key and then walks slowly back to the car while Arsched stares after him.

'Sorry,' I say as he climbs back in. I don't say sorry to Abe. I say sorry to Asif.

'Why should you be sorry?' He turns and looks at me.

'I let him past me, didn't I?' I say.

Asif's got great eyes. 'He saw a weakness, and took it.' He says. And then he turns back around and restarts the car.

When it came to applying to university, I said to Dad – 'The thing is, Dad, I care, but I don't really really care,' and Dad was like – 'What does that even mean?' And I said that I just didn't think – I thought it would probably be quite pointless. Anyway, we actually ended up taking it quite seriously. Dad got really into it. He'd been, Mum hadn't, and nor had his sister – so he was all 'First woman in the family to go to university, that'll be quite something'. So we make lists and more lists, and we go to open days and do ratings and it's quite fun and Dad eventually decides we'll go London School of Economics, we'll go Manchester, we'll go Bristol and then for back-up we'll go Essex and we'll go Southampton. And I'm all – okay – and I – we – spent ages filling in forms – and a few had me up for interviews, and Dad came with me for them too.

The rejections came in one by one. One after the other. Tipping through the box.

Essex took me. The rest... didn't.

And Dad – Dad just said – 'Well, good to have tried, isn't it?' And Essex? Essex.

I scratched his car the night I got the last rejection, from Bristol, three weeks – three weeks that must have been – ago. I went out in the middle of the night with a hair grip and scratched 'cunt' in big letters.

He was really funny the next day. 'Who did this? Who did this?' And Abe, coming to walk me to school, stood with my dad and talked about who could have done it... 'Who could have done it, sir?' He sometimes calls my dad 'sir'. Abe does. And both of them discussed in loud voices who could have written 'cunt' on my dad's car... I've never met Abe's parents – I don't know why...

We drive slowly through Bury Park – now for those of you who don't know Luton – and I don't know why I keep saying that because none of you probably know Luton – it's sort of divided in two – you got your white and black bits and your Asian bits and really the two bits – don't meet, other than with – you know – young people and school. I mean, two separate town centres even. George Street town centre – you'll barely see an Asian face – Bury Park – barely see a white one. True story. And Bury Park has bells in the pavement. That's too complicated to explain. But it's true.

Anyway, Asif is waxing lyrical, as he drives – cruises – I like the word, cruises – with his theory on this kid Iqbal. 'The thing I hate, yeah...' He's saying, and we're all listening '...is the mouthy ones. I mean, they can say what they want to say – I ain't religious, but they can say what they want to say. But do they need to fucking shout about it all the time? "I think this." "I think that." And the young kids growing up, they've got these looks on their faces, man, I ain't ever seen it before. Suicide bombers, the fucking lot of them, and I can say that, and you can't. And this Iqqy...'

'Suicide bomber.' Says J-j-j-Jake. And Asif looks across at him and smiles.

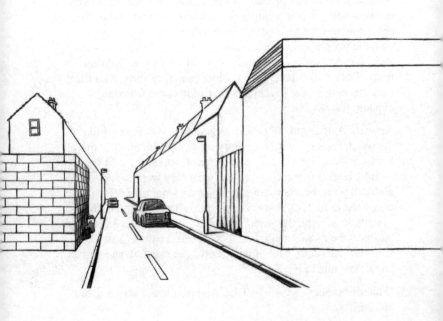

'Yeah. Fucking suicide bomber.' He says. 'Bet he's a Kashmiri fuck too. Never trust a Kashmiri. That's what they say.'

'Where you from, Asif?' Abe asks.

Asif looks at Abe with a shrinking look. 'England, mate,' he says, without a smile. 'What about you, you black devil? You monkey? Where you from?' He laughs then.

'Yeah,' says Abe. With a laugh in his throat. And he doesn't answer the question.

'I suppose it's all about how you interpret things.' I say. Trying to support Abe. And then immediately regretting it. 'Interpret' was the wrong choice of word. Too big a word.

'Is that right?' Asif says, with a smile. And then he looks at me in the mirror and smiles. 'Is it?' he says. He doesn't know what a clarinet is.

'That's right.' I say. And I smile back. And then I look at Abe. His baggy face looking nowhere in particular. Not appreciating my contribution.

'No. No. He'll be a fuck. Iqqy, short for Iqbal. I don't know anyone called Iqbal who isn't a bit fucky.'

'And Asif's a better name, is it?' I say, venturing forward with my dance move. I actually lean forward. I brush against him. I feel the side of my tit touch the side of his arm.

I know what I'm doing.

Asif laughs – he doesn't respond to the tit touch – he just laughs. 'Yeah, love.' He says. 'Asif is a wicked name.' And then he laughs and pulls over to the side of the road and gets out of the car and doesn't invite any of us to go with him. He walks a few paces and then – disappears – inside a butcher's shop. He doesn't explain why or where he's going but that's – well, you probably wouldn't understand why that's a good thing…

We look at each other. The three sort of – well, the three that are waiting. For him. All of us not sure where he's gone. Our leader. 'You okay, Abe?' I ask and J-j-j-Jake turns – taking the piss – 'Yeah, Abe, you okay?' And Abe shoots me a look like him taking the piss is my fault. And I'm all, fuck you and your baggy face. And so I get out of the car and I follow Asif into the shop.

I immediately know I've made a mistake. You know how you do? It's like – I feel my pubic hair crawl back inside me. The butcher's shop – there are only men inside. Men and meat and me. Older men than Asif. And the shop really smells of meat. Because the refrigeration units aren't great and it's hot outside. And everyone else – other than Asif – is wearing those shirts with the apron bits at the front. So they're proper – foreign.

And Asif turns and looks at me and then thinks for a second, he smiles. He indicates to the others with a twist of his head – 'This is Katie,' he says. And they look at me for one or maybe two seconds and then turn back to him. No one says anything. No one speaks at all. They're giving him respect. I don't know why. Maybe he's just one of those guys. Then another man – darker, older, balder, beardier, comes back in – stops when he sees me – and then smoothly hands Asif a bit of paper. And Asif turns and exits past me. And I think for a second and then smile at the men and the meat and follow him out.

'What's that?' Abe asks. Trying not to look at me. When we get back in the car and Asif unfolds the paper.

'His address.' Asif says. 'Iqbal's address.'

'How d'you get that?' Jake asks.

'Small world. I know Asians who know Asians, you get me?' Asif says. And Jake sniggers, and Asif looks proud, and I'm still… And then he winks and smiles at me. Like actually we'd just shared something.

'Knew he was a Kashmiri.' Asif says, his grin even bigger now, restarting the car. 'And when you're looking for a Kashmiri, you ask other Kashmiris. Katie helped.' Abe turns and looks at me with a frown then. And I smile back. And don't question why I helped.

We don't say much as we cruise so Asif turns on the radio. He tries a couple of different buttons until he finds some digital station playing – 'Jump Around' – House of Pain – a 2 a.m. dance-floor classic at a club we used to go to called Paedophiles' Paradise in the town centre – we call it that, don't know the actual name – and it's quite surprising to me and J-j-j-Jake, I think that – well, not just that Asif knows all the words – but that he'd sing along –

She raps (sort of) a line from 'Jump Around' by House of Pain in the style of Asif. Preferably the one that rhymes 'death' with 'breath'.

And then it gets to the chorus – 'jump around jump around' – and suddenly I'm bouncing up and down – 'jump jump jump jump' – I don't mean to – I'm just happy – and Abe looks at me funny – but then Asif starts bumping up and down too and as he lifts off and lands on the accelerator so it makes the car do these little jumps and J-j-j-Jake laughs and joins in. And then Abe is the only one not joined in. And he's gutted but he can't show it.

Asif meets my eyes in the back as we jump jump past the Balti Palace with the boards up and the St George with the old guy outside with whiskers who I always see about the way and who's got this huge bruise on his face at the moment where someone kicked his cheek in, and then we drive through the tower-block gateposts into Marsh Farm. Jump. Jump. 'Or better yet a terminator. Like Arnold Schwarzenegger.'

This area was good once – Dad says – when Vauxhall paid their workers a fiver to find more people to move to the town – when people still wanted to buy Bedford vans. Dad and Mr Harandis talk about it all the time. Harandis blames most of it on the foreigners, he says he knows one guy who bought over five wives on the one Visa. He says it's political correctness gone mad. Dad just nods when he says stuff like that.

Now, Marsh Farm – it's not good – you can see the tower blocks from anywhere in the town: Penhill, Lea Park and Five Springs – and they're – I don't know – Abe was born in Penhill, still lives there, but he doesn't look up at it as we drive past it, because if you belong here… I don't know…

And then Asif pulls on the handbrake, and we realise we're there. Outside the address that was written on the bit of paper given by Kashmiris to Asif the Englishman.

'He's not home.' Asif says. To no one in particular.

Iqqy's house – the one we're – waiting outside of – it's not as bad as the others. There's no rubbish in the front bit and the house has had some sort of paint job at some time, and there are window boxes with green bits poking out in some of the windows.

'How can you tell?' J-j-j-Jake asks.

'His bike is not with the others.' Asif points down the side of the house, there's a metal-grille gate, and through the grille you can see two bikes, neither of them our kid's.

'So now, we… wait?' Abe asks.

Asif adjusts his mirror so he's looking at me again and I look into the mirror to show him I know he's looking and then he turns round and he looks at Abe. 'Actually, Abe, about that, I got the hunger, do us a favour, would you, son? Couldn't go get us some ribs from the shack, could you?'

Abe looks – and then at me – 'Can't Jake go get 'em?'

'Jake's a retard, he'll come back with the wrong order. Besides, I'm asking you. We are chasing down your kid. And I'm paying. You can buy yourself chips with whatever's left.' He hands a fiver to Abe.

Abe looks at him – and then at me. And then gets out of the car and starts walking away. And he looks back at me again. And I just watch. At him walking through this shit estate. Where he's always lived. And I can feel this funny smile on my face.

Asif watches him walk too. He waits 'til Abe turns the corner then turns to me – 'What you with him for?' He asks.

And my stomach does a turn-over. 'Just am, aren't I?'

'What you with a black man for?' He repeats with more detail.

I try and think of a clever response. I can't think of any. 'That doesn't matter.' I say.

Asif turns and looks at where Abe's gone. He's definitely gone. He turns to Jake. 'Fuck off.' And Jake looks at him, and then grins at me and then does fuck off.

And suddenly it's just the two of us in the car.

Just like that.

Just – like that.

Well.

It's a turn-up.

Asif turns and looks at me and then says: 'Why don't you climb through to the front seat?'

And I think about it, and then I do, climb through, but I sort of get stuck because I'm not very good at outdoor pursuits. Outdoor pursuits. And wiggling through seats is always less easy than you think. And so he leans his hand back behind his seat – behind the driver's seat. And he pushes me on the bum so I get through. Reaches around and pushes me on the bum. But he doesn't push me in the normal position on the bum. One of the cheeks or… He pushes me right up the crack. Anyway. I get through.

You know, it was in the paper once that half the arms in the UK were at one point being stored in Marsh Farm. Half of them. In a civil war the capital of Britain would be Luton. And the new palace would be Marsh Farm. Luton – voted the number-one crap town in the UK in 2002. Which makes Marsh Farm the crappest bit of the crappest town in the UK. And it'd have the palace in it.

Luton. Capital of Britain. Where's the Queen? Fuck off. Where's the Queen? Fuck off.

We sit for a moment, me in the passenger seat, him in the driving seat, him looking at me, me not looking at him, suddenly quite shy.

I know what I'm doing.

'You know Abe works in the office where I work?' Asif says. Moving his hand across so it rests on my seat.

'Yeah, he loves you guys – the ones not in the office.'

'Yeah,' Asif says.

'Yeah,' I say.

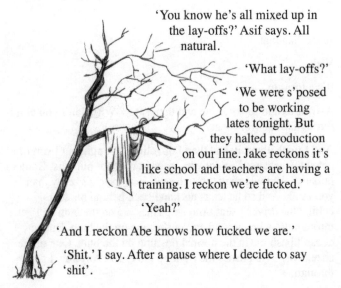

'You know he's all mixed up in the lay-offs?' Asif says. All natural.

'What lay-offs?'

'We were s'posed to be working lates tonight. But they halted production on our line. Jake reckons it's like school and teachers are having a training. I reckon we're fucked.'

'Yeah?'

'And I reckon Abe knows how fucked we are.'

'Shit.' I say. After a pause where I decide to say 'shit'.

'I mean, he ain't – it's not him making the call personally or nothing, I mean, he's the office ball-bag, you know?'

'Yeah.' I say, smiling. 'Yeah. He is.'

'But he's mixed up somehow – he knows. I can tell he knows. And he ain't happy about it, he's well wound up, probably how this whole mess started.' Asif says.

'Yeah.' I say. 'Is this a mess?'

'How do you feel about that?' Asif asks. 'Lay-offs?'

'I don't know.' I say. And I touch his arm again. And he frowns and then smiles at me.

'Take off your knickers.' Asif says. Just like that.

'What?'

'Your knickers. Take them off.' Just like that.

I look at him. I think my hands are shaking. Either that or they're really sweaty. 'I'm not going to fuck you.' I say.

He looks at me like I'm mental. 'I'm not going to fuck you either.' He says. 'I just want you to take off your knickers.'

'Why?' I ask. And he smiles like a greasy kebab salesman.

'That means you're gonna. You ask why, that means you're gonna.'

And I look at him some more and then – maybe because it's hot or – maybe because it's hot – I take off my knickers.

I'm not wearing any tights so it's easy.

They get caught over my shoes and my hands are shaking, but I get them off.

He reaches out a hand to take them from me.

I pray to God they're not stained.

I know what I'm doing. First time I blew Abe… Can't remember the first time I blew Abe. The thing about blowjobs is it's not exactly intimate, is it? You don't even have to look at them. Just their knob. And not even that. I mostly close my eyes to be honest.

He folds them and puts them in his pocket.

He doesn't look at them. And I want to laugh.

'Show me your titty.' He says.

And I still know what I'm doing. First time I got naked for anyone... Must have been two years back. I said I wouldn't fuck him. Like I say, it's been a thing for me. So he made me stand over him while he wanked himself off. Oliver Hartley he was called. We weren't going out. Just 'having fun' he said. Which is kind of similar to what Abe says. He's just using me for sex too – Abe. Oliver Hartley. I thought he was going to splash me so kept my fanny covered. With my hand. While he masturbated. In case any got up me and I got – but he didn't – splash me – he just – splashed his belly. So shows what I know.

I undo my blouse. Shirt. School shirt.

And then take out my tit from my bra. I don't take my bra off. Just lift and... I think that's probably more sexy.

I've got nice nipples. They're probably my most attractive feature. Everyone compliments me on them when I show them to them.

'You're not having my bra. I'm keeping that on. My shirt's see-through basically. I'd be pornographic if I gave that to you.' I say. And Asif nods. Not that giving him my knickers – wa-wah.

'Do you like Abe?' He asks. Looking at my nipple. Just him looking at it makes it hard. And hot. Hot and hard. Though it is hot out.

'Yeah, of course I do. He's my sort of – boyfriend.' I say. I make to put my tit away. He shakes his head. I don't.

'You want to kiss me?' Asif asks.

'I could. Kiss you. If you want.' I say.

And he looks at me. And I don't like it when people look at me. I sometimes like it when people look at me. I don't know how I feel when people look at me.

And he looks me up and down. And he laughs. 'Yeah.' He says. I don't know why it's funny.

'What?' I say.

'Yeah. I could. Couldn't I? Cos I offered. You reckon Jake could if he offered?' His eyes are darker now.

'What?' I say.

Asif winds down the window. 'Jake. Jake.' He calls out. But not loud enough for Jake to hear.

I quickly put my tit away. 'What you doing?' I say. I want to hit him. But in a coy way. I don't hit him. In a coy way or otherwise.

He turns and he looks at me like he understands me entirely. 'You're too easy for me.' He says. His face straight. His body curved.

And just like that, all the spit has drained from my mouth.

He smiles. I don't. But I don't cry.

All the spit has gone.

'Can I have my knickers back?' I say. My lips praying desperately for rain.

He turns and looks at me. His face resets... 'I'll be fine, you know? I'll get other work or I'll – I always wanted to set my own business up, you know? Got some ideas. It's Jake I worry about... ' he says. And then he laughs. 'People look at me and think they know. They fucking don't. Know. I mean, they think you lot... With your universities and your... They think they know.' He says. And his eyes are cold like he could be...

'People look at me,' I say, in reply, 'and think they know. They don't.' Where the fuck is the spit in my mouth?

'Yeah. They do.' Asif says. No smile or frown on his – face – no expression on his – face. 'With you, they know. A scared little girl. A no-knickered cunt.'

And I'm not really digesting that because I've got no spit. 'Can I have my knickers back?' I ask again. I can feel my lips press against each other and make the slapping noise of no moisture.

He smiles at me and then winds down the window. 'Oi.' He shouts. 'Chickenbollocks. Get back in the car.'

Jake comes round the corner from where he's been giving us our privacy. There's an open windscreen in front of me, why didn't I think? Anyone could have looked in. Jake has a – smile. Dispensing – good word – with a fag as he does. I check I'm covered up. I can't really breathe. But it's hot out and stuffy in the car. Asif turns back to me...

'No.' He says. 'You ain't having your knickers back.'

And Jake opens the car door with a smile. He expects me to do something for him.

And I do – I climb out of the door and walk around the back of the car and get in the back seat.

And Asif doesn't look at me.

No. Asif sits and waits for my boyfriend to bring him his ribs.

I started the system as a way of making things feel right. It's like maths basically – you do me wrong for this, I'll do you wrong for that, two plus two equals four, we're all right again. Anything that goes wrong – you put right – by doing wrong. To give an instance, I failed my clarinet grade five – I fucking hate the instrument, I only do it because my parents make me – and I've tried to give it up and school orchestra up but then Dad says it's important – and I should stop going but I'm not very good at saying... how I feel. I'm better at doing. So I dialled a porn number from the paper and left it on. And then I listened in the bathroom – the day they got the phone bill – I listened that night in the bathroom – because my room isn't next to their room, the bathroom is – so I got my duvet and listened in the bathroom as my mum kept saying things like 'Am I not enough for you?' And he was all, 'It wasn't me'. And she was 'Of course it was you, just like it was you who fucked Sarah Almond' – 'Who brought her into it?' And it made me feel better.

Sometimes though… To give another instance, my teacher, year nine, bitch supreme, stands me up in front of the entire lesson – French, this was – and says 'You were talking' and I say I wasn't – though I was – and she says – 'I saw you talking, I'm trying to prepare you for your Key Stage 3s' and I say '(a) I wasn't talking and (b) I couldn't care a less about Key Stage 3s'. Though I could actually, and did quite a lot of revision, which none of my friends did. And she said 'You're a silly little girl,' and then her eyes look at me carefully – looked at my clothes – it was May maybe and I was wearing my skirt, my jumper and my shirt and she says 'Pull up your jumper' and I say 'No, miss, I won't' and she says 'You're wearing a shirt, pull up your jumper'. So I think and then I pull up my jumper showing everyone where I'd rolled up my skirt at the top to make it shorter, which is what everyone did – everyone. And I stood there and everyone was laughing. And she said, 'You may think being cheap will get you by in life, Katie, but I'm here to tell you that it won't, and that a bit of concentration would help you here'. And I knew – I knew – she'd never have done that to the more popular girls, she did it to me because I was just right – not popular enough to be dangerous – not unpopular enough to be bullying. But it was. Bullying. It just was. Anyway, her name was Madame Hanson, and she stank of cats, and I saw her one time, in the laundrette – and I thought – well, first I thought what a scab –

teachers earn enough to get their own washing machines surely – and then I thought it was an opportunity. She was moving her clothes from the washer to the dryer. She put it in the dryer. So I waited 'til she left, she did, and then I went three doors down to the butcher's, bought half a pound of mince, went in to the laundrette, checked no one was looking at me, which they weren't because I look pretty anonymous and opened her machine and added the mince to her drying washing. Every bit of her clothes – it was perfect, she was doing whites – had dried blood and flesh on it by the time she got it out. Apparently she didn't stop screaming for five minutes. She thought she'd accidentally added one of her kittens to her load.

It made me laugh at the time.

Some things I remember really well – some things I really don't – like I can't really tell you what happened when me and Abe got together – I can't tell you where I met him – but I can describe the exact circumstances of every one of the seven other guys I've blown. I can't tell you the name of my first boyfriend – in junior school and he moved – I can remember his face but… But I can tell you the first and last name of every girl that came to my eighteenth. And left my eighteenth. I can't tell you what pieces we're playing in school orchestra at the moment but I can tell you exactly where I was standing when Fat Sheridan – who probably was my only real friend but who I only talked to in the library because the library was safe because no one saw us in there together and I didn't think she was good enough for me – where I was standing when she told me she was leaving school. Good friend. I used to tell her what she looked fat in. I can't tell you what I'm going to do with my life, I can tell you what it felt like in Madame Hanson's last French lesson when she just wouldn't stop crying. And I did that. I'd done that. I did that. And I felt – triumphant. And sick. And triumphant.

We sit there for a good ten – twenty more minutes. Tick. Tick. Tick. Staring at the house of the kid on the bike who knocked Abe's ice cream off its cone. Tick. Tick. Tick.

Abe comes back with Asif's ribs. Tick. Tick. Tick.

We sit there some more. Tick. Tick. Tick.

Asif eats his ribs. Tick. Tick. Tick.

Abe looks at me. I look at Abe. Tick.

It's J-j-j-Jake who suggests it first.

'We could just knock him up.' He says.

'What?' Asif says.

'Knock on his door. One of his family might be in. Wait in there.'

'Have you farted?' Says Asif.

'No.' Says J-j-j-Jake.

'What's your hurry then?'

'It's fucking hot in here. It might be cooler. In there.'

Asif thinks as if for ever – as if this is the hardest decision.

Then he opens the door and walks towards the kid's door. He doesn't answer J-j-j-Jake. He just operates on J-j-j-Jake's plan.

He rings the door once. Hard ring. We get out of the car and follow him like the shit members of a crap gang.

The door opens. A woman. A little Asian woman looks at him. In a sari. In a cloth. She looks at him. Then us. Then back at him.

Asif looks at her. 'Asalamalakum,' he says to her. She says nothing back. She looks scared of him.

Then Jake asks whether we can come in. 'Can we come in, missis?' And Asif shakes his head – 'She don't speak English, bro'. He says.

Then he says something else.

And she says something back.

The truth is – I don't know whether they're speaking Urdu or… you know… whatever. I've never learnt. My dad knows a bit of a few of them. Arabic and Farsi and… But that's for work mainly and the Harandis next door. So they can have their jokes and Dad can pretend not to notice Mr Harandis' racism and Dad can feel multicultural. They buy the *Guardian*, you know. My parents.

And then he says something back. And then she says something. And voices are raised. And she opens the door and lets us in and when Asif turns back to look at us he has a look in his eyes… a look in his eyes… And we go through to their living room. And Asif keeps talking to her, calming her down, making her think it's okay to have us three in her… living room.

We sit in her living room.

And the sofa is too low – lower than an English sofa. My knees are up tit high. And I've got a skirt on with no knickers underneath. So you know, drafty, pornographic… thoughts.

We sit in a row on her too-low sofa. Me. J-j-j-Jake. Smiling. Maybe because he's kind of pleased he's sitting beside me. Or maybe because he's laughing at me because he knows I've just been humiliated. Asif. Abe.

And for some reason – this woman – this boy's mother – she turns on all the electrical things at once. The television. The radio. All the things. And they're all shit electrical things. And the house is faded. It just feels faded. Quite clean. But faded. And with this smell of – musk and sweat that's been left to dry. Not body odour, just musk.

Then she exits – exits – and comes back through with water for us all in a jug. And little glasses and she kneels and pours us all water which she gives to us. And she's too old to kneel really, because she's a proper adult and adults shouldn't kneel in front of people like us. And the water tastes like curry. Or like curry shits actually. The water doesn't taste like curry, it tastes like the smell in the bathroom after you've just had shits after a curry. I'm not…

And then she sits. On a chair.

And Asif moves to sit beside her. On the handle of the chair. Which is not a comfortable place to sit. And she smiles. Nervous. And he says – in English – 'The thing is, you see, your son is a terrorist, and we're here to attach electrodes to his nads... We're gonna burn out his bell-end, aren't we, Abraham?' And Abe nods and looks at me again. His lips are too wet. And Asif turns back to the woman – 'You understand? I can smell your pussy from here, so I know I make you wet, but I don't want you so hot you don't understand – you understand?' The woman nods. She looks at me – the other woman – girl – in the room. And smiles. And her teeth are fucked, all broken and faded and folded on top of each other. And she's got a cloth over her head, and earrings that are too heavy for her ears. And her smile is... desperate. And she just kneeled in front of us.

And Asif thinks he's...

I think most of my problems can be put down to three facts: (i) I was a late developer, (ii) I think too much about what my problems are, (iii) I think too much full stop.

   Pause.

'Can you ask her where her bathroom is?' I say, standing up. Partly because I can't be in the room any more. Partly because I don't sit around in no knickers very much and... Partly because I need a shit.

Asif looks at me and smiles like a wolf – 'You need the toilet, Bunny?' He asks. Bunny? I'm not a – bunny. I'm a scared little girl. I'm a no-knickered...

'Yeah, can you ask her where it is?' I say. I want to scream but I don't. And Asif then talks something to the woman.

She says something back. She smiles again at me. Toothless again.

'It's on the second floor,' Asif says. 'Second right.'

And I look at him and smile. And begin climbing the stairs.

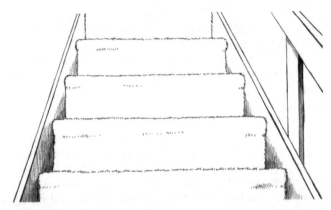

There are shitty photos in shitty frames on the walls. Not that our walls at home aren't any different. Though I have noticed, the older I've got, the less I've featured in our family photos. The less I've...

My mum –

On the top floor facing me is a room with a smell coming from it. Then the bathroom. Then... a door swings open and I...

I've seen my mum cry loads of times.

   Pause.

I first notice the bike, sitting by his wardrobe, then I notice him.

Sitting wedged down by his bed. Like a Jew in Nazi Poland. Hiding. From us.

With his eyes all wide. And he looks at me. And I look at him. All small and young-looking.

And I walk towards him and let myself into his room and shut the door and neither of us are sure what to say so I say: 'You keep the bike up here?'

He nods – his lips are slippy, so his words don't come out properly. 'It's a nice bike. Titanium brakes, you know. People want to nick it.'

I nod.

I think life can be basically divided into two things – feelings – things: suspense – and surprise. Suspense is basically a feeling in your belly – the feeling that things are slowly going bad – surprise is basically a feeling in your brain – a gunshot – a feeling like wooooo. I prefer surprise to suspense. But that's basically because I feel suspense all the time. I mean, all the time, you know? Or – I don't know…

The first time I saw my mum crying is when I wouldn't get her a loaf of bread from the shop down the road. I was watching tel-evision. I wish I'd kept a diary. Just for things like that. She's quite pathetic really. My mum. And not that pretty. I see a lot of me in her. Though I don't cry.

And he says 'I met you, open day, London School of Eco-nomics.'

I don't remember.

He says 'We were in same session. On American military history. And they paired us, and then we ended up ont same train home. Though I don't know if you noticed me. I noticed you.' He says. I don't remember him. 'Don't tell.' He says.

'You were at my LSE open day?'

'Yeah.' I look at his eyes to check whether he's lying.

'You spat at him. You spat at my boyfriend.'

'He knocked me off my bike.' He says, surprised-sounding. 'You were there.'

And I decide to ignore that. 'Why did you spit?'

'You do what you do, right?' He says. Like a kid from Marsh Farm. He's kind of funny-looking. Close up his hair really is too long. And his mouth's a funny shape. And he really is scrawny. He doesn't pay enough attention to his appearance. He's got loads of spots.

'Do you?' I ask. 'Do you do what you do?'

And he looks at me and he looks right through me. 'I do.'

The last time I saw Mum cry... was... I found her on my bed. And she was crying. 'I'm just so worried about you.' And I said 'Why?' And she looked at me and said she didn't know. I mean, is that an answer for a mum to give?

I had a dream once – about a moment where I stuck a tube through my eye and sucked my own brain out. Using my own mouth. It wasn't a nightmare. It was a dream. I don't like thinking. I don't like thinking. I don't like thinking. I don't like thinking. I don't like thinking. I don't like thinking. I don't like thinking. I don't like thinking. I don't like thinking. I don't like thinking. I don't like thinking. I don't like thinking. I don't like thinking. I don't like thinking. I don't like thinking. I don't like thinking. I don't like thinking. I don't like thinking.

But I do. Think. All the time.

   Pause.

When Mum said that. Thing. I tried to think of a payback. A way of levelling the accounts. I thought of some stuff – replacing her Echinacea with – um – laxatives but that wasn't... No. Turned out, I couldn't think of anything.

   Pause.

'Did you get in?' I ask – softly – really softly – 'to LSE?'

He looks at me. 'Yeah.' He says, with an itch of his face. 'But I'm not going.'

'Oh.' I say. 'Where are you going?'

'Oxford.' He says.

And I look at him and I slowly raise my skirt. To show him where I'm knickerless.

And he looks at me surprised.

And I look at him.

'Have you got an erection?' I ask.

And he says nothing, just nods.

And I look at him and I let go of my skirt.

And I'm imagining two futures.

One where I shout down the stairs. 'Abe. Asif. He's up here.' And they come charging up and drag him downstairs with his mum shouting 'No, no' and 'I'll call the police'. And no one cares about the police or otherwise, they just want to tear this kid – hurt this kid – and they hit him and they open his mouth and make him eat pavement and then they kick the back of his head – so his jaw is broken almost in two – so the pavement goes – so the blood slowly grows… In a pool that becomes a pond that becomes a sea.

None of the fights I've seen have ever got anywhere. I can't imagine a fight that gets somewhere. His mum shouting 'No, no'. All – 'No, no'. 'No, no'.

And the other – I imagine the other future where – nothing – happens.

And I look at him.

And I look at him.

And I look at him.

And I've got this funny look on my face and he – finally – he finally says 'What?' But he says it in a whisper again.

And I say 'I'm thinking'.

And he says 'About what?'

And I say 'Maths'.

And he just frowns…

Pause.

And then I shake my head at him – imperceptibly – good word – and back out – of the room.

And I – go down – the stairs.

I don't go to the toilet.

I go down – stairs.

And I look at the door. I stand looking at it for ages. The door. The door.

Then I turn around – and return – to the living room.

To sit with the others.

To wait for the situation to be resolved one way or the other.

To wait for them to find him or…

I chose – suspense. Or maybe I chose to – free him?

Maybe I'm…

Maybe I'm doing…

And Abe is sitting there, and Asif is sitting there, and J-j-j-Jake is sitting there and Asif looks up at me and smiles, and there is a space beside J-j-j-Jake which is where I was sitting before but I stand in front of Abe and him and Asif and J-j-j-Jake scooch up so there's a space beside him – Abe – I'm sitting by – I sit by Abe on the sofa and as I sit he sort of absent-mindedly pats my hand. Like he likes me. Or was worried about me or something…

Yeah.

They'll probably…

And I'm all… I'm all.

I'm all. All. You know? All.

But I'm pretty sure no one notices.

The End.

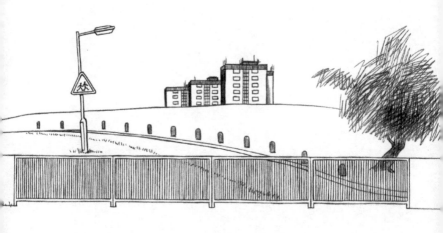

RED CAR, BLUE CAR

Red Car, Blue Car was first performed at the Bush Theatre, London, as part of their Where's My Seat? season, in June 2011, with the following cast:

PHIL	Hugo Speer
MARIE	Nina Sosanya
Director	Tamara Harvey
Designers	Amy Cook and Lucy Osborne

Characters

PHIL
MARIE

Also:

TOM, *non-speaking*
FIONA, *non-speaking*
MARK, *non-speaking*

There are three chairs and a lot of crap on the stage. PHIL *sits in the middle chair.*

TOM *enters carrying a giant strawberry.* MARIE *enters behind him with a very small tub of cream which she eats with a spoon. He seems a little lost. He exits the stage.* MARIE *thinks and then sits on a chair beside* PHIL.

PHIL. There is a woman sitting with a boy with swollen eyes. He must be no more than ten. She's holding his arm for him – cradling it in her lap. And he keeps looking at it as if he's afraid it will disappear. Like it's not attached to him. A guy with a bloodied bar napkin taped to his head walks past them. He holds eye contact with the mother. Then wobbles and moves on. A woman sits playing with her phone and looks at nothing as she gently cries. An old black woman sits in the corner waiting for news. I keep expecting someone to ask – what are you here for? No one asks what am I here for… A woman comes rattling past, her man rattling beside her. She's pregnant. He thinks he is. Showing off as he shouts encouragement. Looking to the nurses for audience appreciation. You're doing fucking great. You're doing fucking great.

MARIE. 'You fucking do it. You fucking do it.' I push him across the bed with a smile and he looks at me with a capacious grin. Do I mean capacious? He takes the basketball and puts it under his T-shirt and smiles and goes 'Big Bertha' – it's sort of a name – it's not a name – 'Big Bertha' – you have to say it like a fairground attendant to really get the use out of it 'Big Bertha' – followed by one of his laughs – gna gna gna gna – he laughs like a cartoon character. Anyway, then he hands it to me. Like it's a present – a gift – a present. And I look at it – think and then I put it – I put the basketball up my top. And I'm nervous for some reason. And he says 'you look beautiful' – and he's got the eyes he sometimes does – 'you're beautiful' and I say 'damn, really, if I knew it'd be this easy I'd have got pregnant years ago' and he says 'you look beautiful.' And I say 'Okay. All I've done is let you fuck me and pissed on a stick. But okay.' 'You look beautiful' he repeats and I smile and I say 'Okay. Okay. You're getting boring now.' And then he says 'Big Bertha' and I laugh – he laughs Gna Gna Gna Gna – and I hit him.

PHIL. The mother and child are called. She delicately moves his arm as they stand together. But it hurts him and he looks at her like she's caused the pain. She smiles like she doesn't mind. A young man comes in and walks delicately up to reception – they ask what's wrong he says I think I need a private consultation, the receptionist nods at him and says someone will come right out to take his details. When they do it's behind a curtain. And I never see him again.

MARIE *picks up a basketball from the debris and puts it under her top. She turns around – humming 'The Stripper' and doing a weird dance move.*

Reception – two women with too much make-up on trying to look like they understand everything. I think about my wife and daughter. The man with the bloodied napkin is called and taken through. A young black woman comes in and sits beside the old black woman waiting for news. She's been crying. The old woman hasn't. They barely talk. A man of my age comes in and tells the reception something and then sits gently swaying holding his gut. I won't see him taken through. There are the sounds of sirens coming and sirens going but I never see a paramedic. The show-off man comes through and starts making loud phone calls to everyone he knows. It's so fucking exciting, he declares, so exciting. I'm over the fucking moon, fucking moon, we both are. Yes. She's just birthing the placenta now. Then a doctor emerges. Elegantly peeling off slightly bloodied latex gloves as he walks. He's approaching the reception desk. He talks to the prettier receptionist. All prettiness is relative. She touches his hand as they talk. He tells her the RTA is dead. And that's all I need to hear.

MARIE. We met on – the internet. Not a thing I'm particularly proud of. I'd like to say we met on a cultural-exchange project in Cairo. Or dancing in a nightclub in Brixton to heavy heavy beats. Or at the zoo – I was with my niece, he was with his nephew – we met at the monkey compound when they got chatting, we were embarrassed at first then he did a monkey impression, and I was like a squidgy banana in his hands.

PHIL. I leave the hospital via the front entrance and stand smoking a cigarette – my wife doesn't like me smoking. And then I – then I –

PHIL *exits the stage*.

MARIE. But we didn't meet at any of those places, we met on the internet. The home of porn, Wikipedia, humiliation and loneliness. I am a woman – click – looking for a man – click – my age is – click – my income bracket is – click – my preferred age for him is – click click click – my preferred income bracket is – click click click click – tell us about yourself – click click click click click – what do you do for a living – click click click click click click – what do you like to do in your spare time – click click click click click – where do you see yourself in ten years – click click click click click click – where do you see yourself in one hundred years – click click click click click click – are you tall, medium, short – do you have a small, medium or large breasts – do you have sticky pointy round or slightly darkish nipples – do you have any special skills you can do with said nipples – have you ever fellated a horse? I met one man – Guardian Soulmates – lovely, fresh, gentle, Guardian Soulmates – asked me to wear a muzzle – how do I find out if you're my Guardian Soulmate? How do I know if you're the person drawn into dating via a left-leaning website who I could spend the rest of my life with? Oh, I know... I'll get you to wear a muzzle. The secret – and I was stupid not to guess this – the secret to soulmating – for life – is muzzling – for life. True. Story. Yes, there were – there are – some men – some male daters – who need to die – and I did briefly consider becoming a notorious Match dot com murderess – the notorious Match dot murderess. Different profiles, different internet cafés, tell them to meet me in a variety of places, offer to let them meat me – M–E–A–T – see what I've done – yeeah – take them home – drug them – then tie them up and gently skin their penis and watch them while they bleed out in the bath.

TOM *re-enters and then exits.*

Matt was the seventeenth I met. I briefly did call him Mr Seventeen and then he asked what that meant and I said that – I said I didn't want to explain. He said he enjoyed how old-fashioned internet dating was – the exchange of letters, the occasionally chaperoned first date, the gentle discovery of each other. But the truth is – was – is that Matt was just as lonely as I was. Big Bertha and Mr Seventeen.

FIONA *enters the stage and sits beside* MARIE.

'Let's go for a drink' he says. 'Yeah. Let's go do some shots. The baby will like that.' I say. He laughs. Gna gna gna. 'Okay. Then let's go for a coffee. An ice cream.' 'It's one a.m.'

PHIL *re-enters and sits beside* FIONA. *He's carrying a thermos. He pours himself a coffee.*

'Then let's go for a walk, I can't sleep, I'm not going to sleep now and nor are you – let's go for a walk.'

And I say – 'Okay.'

PHIL. The streets are quiet. It's five a.m. A man ambles past. With a gait. Red car. Blue car. He looks at me as I pass him. He smells of mustard and wet newspaper and dick. Black car. Yellow car. Blue car. Blue car. A woman in a business skirt walks too quickly for her shoes. Each step involves a slight slip. Guttaging guttaging guttaging. A man listens to his phone dressed in overalls. Not walking too quickly. Not music. Some speech radio or – comedy podcast – he smiles as he passes. Not at me.

PHIL *drinks his coffee.*

MARIE. And he folds his arm in mine. And I say 'what are we doing out here, it's cold,' and he says, 'we're being insane together. We're celebrating.' And I say 'Okay.'

PHIL. Blue car. Red car. Blue car. Green car. Orange car. Red car. Blue car. Two men walk together. Identical to look at. But saying nothing. Both have a newspaper tucked under the same arm – both walk with – big steps. Blue car. Red car. Black car. Blue car. Black car. Blue car. White car. I watch the white car as it travels away. Whoever's driving it has it in

too low a gear. The car is screaming. A Pakistani gentleman
comes out of a shop rubbing his hands and pulls down an
awning. He's selling cheap fruit. I want to say something
racist to him. I buy an apple. A red car, a blue car, a grey car,
a second red car. I take a bite of the apple. I put it in the bin.

FIONA. Carrots. Lettuce. Cucumber. Plums. Oranges. Apples.

MARIE. He'd asked me to move in with him six hundred times
before I consented. Because he – but one time I woke up in
the morning and he was just staring at me – staring at me – I
mean, I'm pretty – *but the way he looked at me. He looks at
me* – he takes out two small Club chocolate bars from his
pocket. 'Took them from the kitchen' he says 'before I left.'
We walk past a woman who is just talking to herself
underneath her breath.

FIONA. Onions. Bananas. Bread. Beans. Fish? Fish. Beef? No.
Fish. Fish.

PHIL. I work for the RAC. I work late. People still need the RAC
after dark. We actually do an important job. I handle overflow
– times when we can't get to a car in time, when we need a
local garage to handle it – I have a database of garages – I run
a small team. The AA describes itself as the fourth emergency
service. We aren't so bold. But it's still important. If I do a
good job, people's lives are better. And when… and when…

MARIE. We walk past this old derelict ice-cream parlour – from
the days when this town was a seaside resort rather than a
shithole. And he says – hold on. And he moves a wheelie bin
under the – and he says – gna gna – I'm going to get you that
strawberry – there's a wooden strawberry on top of the ice-
cream parlour – he's feeling full-up and masculine – my seed
did the deed. I am an internet dater no more. I am a man. And
he climbs on the wheelie bin and uses it to attempt to get onto
the window ledge. 'I'm going to get that strawberry as a first
gift for our child.' He gets a sort of grip on the window ledge
but he doesn't – he can't pull himself up. He's trying as hard
as he can but he doesn't quite have the muscles for it. See me
tear my T-shirt off and reveal my belly. He looks like the time
we went to France and he spoke French the entire time and
when we were leaving our hotel our hotelier hugged him and

told him he enjoyed having us as his guests. 'Matt' I say.
'Matt' I say. 'I don't need the stupid wooden strawberry.' I
say. And he smiles and says 'Okay.' And he laughs – gna –
gna – gna. And then he puts his hand back in mine. And the
strawberry stays safe on top of the ice-cream parlour.

PHIL. I walk over a bridge. I stop in the middle. I stop in the
middle. A plane soars through the air in the skies above me.
A blue. Plane. I look out over everything and take a breath.
Then I take another breath. Then I take another breath. Then
I take another breath. My dad told me once he wished he
could hug me. Then I take another breath. I had a dog once
who came back to life. We were halfway through burying
him when we realised he was still alive. Then I take another
breath. Then I take another breath. Blue cars. Red cars. The
smell of a cheap morning. I need to get my car. I've left it in
the hospital car park. Yellow cars. Blue cars. Red cars. Black
cars. I take another breath.

MARIE. 'Martin.' 'Martin?' 'Yeah. Martin.' 'Why?' 'Two
reasons. One, Martin Keown.' 'Martin Keown, you want to
name your child after Martin Keown?' 'He was a very solid
player for us.' 'Solid?' 'Second reason – George Martin.'
'We are not calling our child Martin.' 'Why not?' 'A – it's a
shit name. B – Matt, Marie and Martin, we'll be called the
fucking Ms.' 'Okay. Henry.' 'After Thierry Henry?' 'Not just
– Henry Bloomfeld.' 'The Bond villain.' 'The fucking
brilliant Bond villain.' 'Sounds too posh, a kid called Henry
will get the shit beaten out of him.' 'My child will never be
bullied.' 'I was bullied.' 'Yeah, but you're dead spiky. He'll
be popular and funny.' 'Well… whatever… These names
sound like the names of people that died in the war. And we
don't know if it's a girl.' 'That's the advantage of Henry and
Martin – Henrietta and Martine. Job done.' Gna gna gna. 'I
actually physically hate you right now.' 'Yeah? Well, I've
never loved you more.' He laughs. Gna gna gna. I hit him.
I'm sort of going with it. I'm half-acting. He knows it. He's
very good at sensing me. He starts to run away. 'Martine.'
'Henrietta.' He shouts as he runs across the road – 'Spiky,
I'm fucking spiky' I spit – as he is hit hard by a Volvo Estate.

She makes a noise from the back of her throat.

PHIL. My favourite story from the Bible. Lot at the gates of
Sodom and Gommorah. Innkeeper. He sees some angels
approaching. He sees some – it doesn't matter.

MARIE. A fucking Volvo Estate.

She makes a noise from the back of her throat.

And I watch him as he slides up on the bonnet and then
down and then – I watch as the Volvo – drives – Volvo drives
– Volvo drives –

PHIL. And I'm home. We have a kitchen clock. It ticks loudly.
She brought it. I sit and watch it tick as I eat my bacon and
eggs. The bacon isn't cooked properly. It's still soggy in its
own fat. I should have made beans to go with it not eggs.
Beans hide the worst in any meal. I pour – I pour a glass of
orange juice to mask the glistening taste of bacon descending
into my belly. My daughter comes downstairs. It's seven
thirty a.m. She's in her nightie. The nightie is too short for
her. It's effectively a large T-shirt.

MARIE. 'What's his name? Can you tell me his name? What's
his name? Can you tell me his name?' 'Can you wait here.
Can you wait here.' They repeat their instructions three
times. They constantly turn the instructions over in their
mouths. What's his name? What's his name?

FIONA *gets up and leaves the stage. The middle chair is
now empty.*

What's his name?

PHIL. She bends to get a bowl out of the bottom cupboard. She
clangs the enamel of the bowl as she pulls it out. She pours
corn flakes inside. 'You're up early' she declares. 'Yeah' I
say. She smiles a slightly goofy grin and then changes it to a
more sophisticated one. She's at that age. She's fourteen.
'You got anything good at school today?' I ask her. She turns
– surprised – she thinks – and then says 'No, not really.' I nod
'And everything's okay,' I ask 'with you?' She frowns and
then smiles 'Yeah, everything's okay, Dad.' I nod. And turn
back to my undercooked bacon. She thinks then sits beside
me. We eat in silence. Her breakfast is louder than mine.

MARIE. The clock-ticks sound loud. Tick tick. I get my phone
out – tick tick – phone – out – phone – out – and try to work
out who to call. Tick tick tick. I feel like I'm fourteen. Tick
tick tick. I can't call – I can't call… I look around the waiting
room. Tick tick tick. A mum and her kid. Tick tick. He's
broken his arm. Tick tick tick tick. A drunk cunt who's
wrapped his smashed head in bar napkins. Tick tick tick tick.
An older woman and her child waiting for news. Tick tick tick
tick tick tick tick. A white-faced man sitting lonely as he – and
then this pregnant couple come through and I feel myself want
to vomit and the man with her loves her so much… Tick tick
tick tick tick tick tick. It feels so fucking average. And I can
feel my heart beat through my neck. Tick tick tick tick tick
tick tick tick tick tick tick tick tick tick tick tick tick tick.

PHIL. My wife is not surprised to see me. She's still in bed,
reading her book.

MARIE. Tick tick tick tick tick tick tick tick tick tick tick tick
tick tick tick tick tick tick tick.

PHIL. She's taken to reading her book in the morning rather
than the evening because she says she's too tired in the
evening now that she's old. She's not old. She'll get up just
before our daughter needs to be in school and drive her there.
Still smelling of bed.

MARIE. Tick tick tick tick tick tick tick tick tick tick tick tick
tick tick tick tick tick tick tick. I go to the bathroom. I piss
for something to do. And I touch my belly, and I want to put
two fingers in my belly button and tear myself open and pull
the mucal matter out. Tick tick tick tick tick tick tick tick tick
tick tick tick tick tick tick tick tick tick tick.

PHIL. We're not a sociable family in the morning, we all need our
own space. She'll have her breakfast when she's home after
driving our daughter. 'Late one was it?' She asks. Yes. I say. A
couple of the lads didn't come in so I had to take their shifts.

MARK *enters and stands at the back*.

MARIE. No. *I see him enter reception*.

PHIL. I nod.

MARIE. No. *The receptionist points at me*. *No*. No. He approaches with a – look. I feel my belly tear. I feel my anus clench.

MARK *walks behind* FIONA*'s chair but doesn't get on it*.

PHIL. A couple of lads didn't come in.

From offstage there is the sound of a baby crying.

MARIE. No. No. No.

PHIL. She asks whether I'm okay, I look pale. I just nod. I had a bit of trouble with the Volvo I say, a slight accident. I say.

MARIE. No. No. No. No. No.

MARK. I'm so sorry for your loss.

PHIL. Bang.

MARIE. No. No.

PHIL. Bang. Bang. Bang. Bang. I drove – I drove – what are you supposed to do but drive – he walked out in front of me – he walked out in front of me.

MARK. I'm so sorry. We did everything we could.

PHIL. I did everything I could. Apart from stop. He wasn't alone. I checked that much. There was a woman with him.

MARIE. No. No. No.

MARK. Now can I just talk to you about – this isn't going to be easy – but I need to talk to you about organ donation.

PHIL. She looks up then, bang, suddenly, bang, you had a car accident she says. Bang. Slight. I say. I lost my bearings slightly on the Plymouth road – bang – and drove off road pranged the Volvo on a bush I say – nothing serious I say. But I may need to borrow your car I say.

MARK *exits*.

While I get mine seen to. She says okay, you had a car accident? I say, again, nothing serious. She doesn't look convinced. I start to take my clothes off and get into bed. I strip naked. Just for a few days I say. She says you can have it as long as you need. I climb into bed beside her. She takes me in her arms. Are you sure you're okay? She says. I say yes. She strokes my body. I let her. She says 'You're damp with sweat.' I smile. She strokes my body. A car accident? I'm fine. I smile. I begin to stiffen. She smiles.

She gently begins to touch me. I'll be late for the school run she says. I know. I say. Doesn't matter. A car accident? She says. As she puts me inside her with a generous smile. Yeah. I say. I love you, she says. I love you too I say.

There is the longest pause we can sustain.

MARIE *stands and walks through the props. She picks up a box. From the box she unwraps a blue plane. She reveals nothing of herself. She just looks at the plane. She just looks at it.*

She stays standing. PHIL *stays sitting. Until the end of the play.*

MARIE. The nurses say – the nurses say – do you want five minutes? Five. And I say – I just smile and nod and say yes. And they say we'll be just – we'll be just out here.

PHIL. I've never been good at feeling safe.

MARIE. He still has the mask. The oxygen mask. And I – stand there – with this masked man in front of me and I – recognize the eyes behind the mask and sort of – walk towards it – *and I lift the mask* – then I bend and reluctantly I – kiss his mouth, and I can taste – him and – and I kiss it – enquiringly – again – and I can taste this sour – sour – I couldn't tell you where it's from but this sour – this sour – sour – and then I kiss him again – passionately – as if my whole life – my whole life – my whole life – my whole life – my whole life – my whole life… And then I realise what I'm tasting – I'm tasting – blood. And I feel something – stir – inside of me.

She does something no one has ever done before.

She does it again.

She waits.

Blackout.

MYDIDAE

For Sophie Gardiner

Mydidae was first performed at Soho Theatre, London, on 5 December 2012, with the following cast:

MARIAN	Phoebe Waller-Bridge
DAVID	Keir Charles

Director	Vicky Jones
Designer	Amy Jane Cook
Lighting Designer	Jack Williams
Composer and Sound Designer	Isobel Waller-Bridge

The production subsequently transferred to the Trafalgar Studios, London, on 5 March 2013.

Characters

MARIAN
DAVID

ACT ONE

Scene One

MARIAN *enters the bathroom. She's wearing overlarge headphones.*

She's talking business French aloud. She's wearing knickers and a Minnie Mouse T-shirt. She's just slept in them.

MARIAN. Est-ce qu'il y a un service de bus pour aller à Paris?

Est-ce qu'il y a un service de bus pour aller à Paris?

Beat.

C'est bien le bus pour Versailles?

C'est bien le bus pour Versailles?

She picks up a toothbrush and begins brushing her teeth.

She continues saying French aloud.

C'est bien le train pour Lille?

C'est bien le train pour Lille?

She brushes her tongue.

DAVID *enters. He's on the phone. He's in a pair of grey boxer shorts.*

She stops talking. He doesn't acknowledge her.

DAVID. I'm going to start with that…

I'm going to start with that…

He looks at her. He makes a signal. She doesn't understand it and laughs. He frowns.

Because I want to open hard…

If I start with that…

Well. It's a matter of opening hard.

She washes the toothbrush and puts it away.

She turns off her iPod. She listens to his call.

She sits on the side of the bath.

She thinks and then takes out some dental floss.

She begins to floss. He looks at her as she does. He smiles.

She smiles back. She starts to sexily floss. It's a hard thing to do sexily. She laughs.

If we don't open hard...

It's not about what's right or what's – right.

He looks at her. He covers the phone.

I don't know why you floss after you brush your teeth.

MARIAN. I don't know either. Is he being a dick?

He goes back to his phone.

DAVID. It's my pitch. It's my pitch.

...

Yes. Of course it's our pitch. It's our pitch. But it's my pitch to lead.

He covers the phone.

Flossing creates shit in your mouth.

MARIAN. Ya-huh and I can taste it if I do it before.

DAVID. Taste what?

MARIAN. The shit.

He goes back to the phone.

DAVID. I'm the pitcher. That's all I mean by that. I'm the pitcher and... that makes me the leader.

I know I sound like a tosser.

I'm just getting words – mixed up.

No. I won't.

He covers the phone.

Still. It doesn't make logical sense.

MARIAN. You're talking to me?

DAVID. Yeah.

MARIAN. You don't make logical sense. He's being a dick, right?

DAVID *smiles. He talks into the phone.*

DAVID. Yeah... Yeah... Well, complain about it if you want to...

Kiss me.

MARIAN *laughs.*

MARIAN. You're talking to me?

He smiles. She does kiss him. With a smile. Gently. On the mouth. He breaks off and talks immediately into the phone. She frowns.

DAVID. Yeah. Yeah.

I know. I know.

MARIAN *thinks. She turns her iPod back on. She begins to recite French again.*

MARIAN. On est bien en direction d'Avignon?

On est bien en direction d'Avignon?

DAVID. I...

He exits. She looks after him. She stops. A thoughtful expression on her face. She looks in the mirror. She smiles. Then she doesn't.

MARIAN. On est bien en –

Then she exits.

Then DAVID re-enters. Now off the phone.

He begins to take a piss. It's a long piss.

He sings gently, 'If You're Happy and You Know It.'

He stops singing.

DAVID. I can't smell the asparagus.

MARIAN (*off*). What?

DAVID. The asparagus.

From last night.

I can't smell it.

Does that mean it was good or bad asparagus?

MARIAN re-enters the bathroom.

MARIAN. I don't know.

DAVID. Is it one of those things?

Apparently the more that beetroot reddens your piss, the better it is.

The best beetroot turns your piss to almost blood colour.

MARIAN. Is that right? What did he want?

DAVID. Stuff.

She starts the bath. She checks the temperature of the water.

He sings a little more. Just hmming it. Not emitting actual words.

He finishes. He shakes. He puts away.

MARIAN. It's taking longer and longer to heat up nowadays. Is that the boiler or the tap?

He washes his hands. She flushes the toilet.

I can't smell it either. The asparagus.

DAVID. No.

DAVID opens the bathroom cabinet and takes out some shaving foam and a razor.

MARIAN. So that's something…

DAVID *laughs.*

He lathers up.

He begins to wet-shave.

Men always look so stupid with shaving foam on their face.

DAVID. Do men?

MARIAN. What's wrong with that?

DAVID. How many men have you seen? Me. Your dad. Who else?

MARIAN. You resent my use of the plural?

DAVID. A bit.

MARIAN. Because it feels incorrect or because it makes me sound like a whore?

DAVID *takes some shaving foam from his face and carefully places it on* MARIAN's *nose. She lets him with a grin.*

DAVID. Suits you.

MARIAN. Thank you.

DAVID *squirts some more shaving foam and carefully applies it to* MARIAN's *arse. She lets him. With a grin. He squirts some direct onto her arse. She now has a bunny tail.*

DAVID. *Really* suits you.

MARIAN. Thank you.

DAVID *looks her up and down.*

DAVID. Are you putting on weight?

MARIAN. No.

DAVID. It's fine if you are. You're skinny as a thing.

I'm just interested.

MARIAN. No. I'm not.

DAVID. I'm just interested.

I think you are. You should get yourself weighed.

MARIAN. I do – I actually weigh myself.

I'm not putting on weight.

DAVID. I'm just interested. Like I say, it's not a… You're so thin.

A bit of weight…

MARIAN. I'm not.

DAVID *thinks and then doesn't push it.*

MARIAN *puts the plug in the bath. It begins to fill.*

DAVID. Paul wants to start with the gross output. Save the sales figures till the end. Leave on a high.

MARIAN. You want to start with the figures?

DAVID. Start with a bang. Work backwards from there.

MARIAN. I think I'd trust your judgement over Paul's.

DAVID. You are putting on weight.

Your arse.

It has more flesh on it.

Beat.

MARIAN. You're not exactly thin.

DAVID. You are thin. It's not a bad thing.

I'm just interested.

I like watching your body change.

Beat.

MARIAN. You're balding.

DAVID. I like watching your body change. Is it ass or arse?

MARIAN. I'm the same weight I always am. You're losing hair daily. Or at least monthly.

DAVID. Your body is reapportioning it then. Less on the arms.

More in the ass. The ass is definitely bigger. I like it. It's an age thing.

MARIAN (*sharp*). 'It's an age thing'?

DAVID. What? Yeah, I don't mean that like…

MARIAN. Full of compliments this morning, aren't you?

DAVID. I like your arse with a bit more flesh on it. I think it's arse not ass.

Before I met you, I was quite into fat girls actually.

MARIAN. You've told me before.

DAVID. Have I?

MARIAN. You had a theory, when you were drunk, that fat-girl vaginas were warmer than thin-girl vaginas. You asked me what I thought.

DAVID. What did you think?

MARIAN. It took me a while to make up my mind and then I tipped a Ribena over your pyjamas.

DAVID. Oh, that night.

MARIAN. Yeah. That night.

DAVID. Didn't we… after…

MARIAN. Yeah. We did. Ribena does funny things to a girl.

He smiles. She smiles. They're remembering something.

MARIAN takes a towel from the rack and uses it to get the shaving foam off the back of her knickers.

You were shaking in your sleep last night.

DAVID. Was I?

MARIAN. Shaking and grinding your teeth. Like a scared dog.

DAVID. Talking too?

MARIAN. No. No talking. Mum wants us to come by on Sunday.

DAVID. Yeah?

We're probably going to be busy that day.

MARIAN. I thought so.

DAVID. You're beautiful. You have a beautiful body. It's
fantastic.

I'll never get tired of it.

MARIAN. Thanks for the forewarning.

DAVID. What? You're strange.

Beat.

MARIAN. Am I?

They slip into silence.

I know.

Pause.

I quite fancy a Ribena now.

DAVID *finishes wet-shaving. He washes his face in the dirty
water.*

He looks at her carefully.

I had that dream again.

She sits on the toilet and pulls down her knickers.

DAVID. Did you?

MARIAN. With some slight variations. I was standing –
naked –

DAVID. Obviously.

MARIAN. In front of this huge burning fire. In the middle of
the countryside.

And my feet were buried in concrete.

And I had this desperate need – this overwhelming need – to
begin to pee.

DAVID. Obviously.

She begins to pee. She laughs.

MARIAN. As if by magic…

DAVID. As if by magic…

MARIAN. Anyway, then I noticed these people – these grass
people – these people made of grass – were watching me and
were all masturbating – they can't have been more than three
inches high but it was clear what they were doing – and I
was – disgusted and started to shout at them all – and then
you rode in on a small horse – to save me – and…

I was delighted and you started fighting the grass people but
they totally overwhelmed you and slit your throat.

And so I was stuck there – for eternity – desperate to pee –
naked – in front of these masturbating grass people.

DAVID. I had a dream too – I was being blown by a girl with
really goofy teeth – like splaying-out-in-all-directions sort of
teeth – like that guy from the Bash Street Kids.

MARIAN. I think it's weird that you don't remember your
dreams.

DAVID. At least I don't have weird dreams.

Beat.

MARIAN. At least you don't.

DAVID. How small was my horse?

MARIAN. I don't know.

DAVID. Was it – I don't know – pygmy-sized?

MARIAN. You think it was a metaphor?

Because you were also murdered.

By three-inch masturbators.

DAVID. I don't know.

He sits on the edge of the bath.

She stands and then sits on his lap.

This isn't comfortable.

MARIAN. We just need to get through today...

Beat.

DAVID. I've got that pitch...

MARIAN. No. I mean...

DAVID. Yeah. I knew what you meant. I just meant it'll be harder for you because I've got my pitch.

MARIAN. Thanks for the concern.

DAVID. I'm not...

MARIAN. I know.

They sit for ages.

How big was my horse?

DAVID *just looks at her.*

Don't listen to Paul. Do your thing.

Whatever feels right in the room.

I don't know anyone better at sensing a room than you.

DAVID. Yeah. That is... Yeah.

Pause. He looks at her carefully.

Sometimes I really don't know what you're thinking...

MARIAN. Sometimes I don't know what you're thinking either.

DAVID. I'd like to – open your brain and climb inside.

MARIAN. Crack it like a nut.

DAVID. Crack it like a nut and then climb inside – to the soft gooey –

MARIAN. My brain isn't gooey – it's rubbery –

DAVID. To the soft rubbery inside...

MARIAN. And it smells vaguely of honey. My brain smells of honey.

DAVID. To the soft rubbery – honey-smelling insides beneath.

MARIAN *looks at* DAVID, *who looks back.*

MARIAN. No.

You wouldn't.

Beat.

DAVID. Yes. I would.

MARIAN. You've got such strong hands.

I like your hands.

It was probably a big horse.

Pause.

DAVID. Should I cancel the pitch? I didn't mean it'd be easier...

MARIAN. I know what you meant.

DAVID. I shouldn't be going in today, should I?

MARIAN. What do you think the masturbating grass people meant?

DAVID. Kiss me.

MARIAN. Okay.

MARIAN *does.*

DAVID. Kiss me again.

MARIAN. Okay.

They kiss again.

They begin to kiss more passionately. He rubs her arse, and then he reaches under it.

Really?

He begins to masturbate her.

Really?

DAVID. Yeah.

MARIAN. You're going to be late for your meeting...

DAVID. I've got time.

He kisses her again. She breaks off again.

MARIAN. You are.

DAVID. No.

It's the morning. I always cum quicker in the morning.

MARIAN. Romantic.

He kisses her again. He breaks off with a laugh.

DAVID. Masturbating grass people…

MARIAN. Says the man who always cums quicker in the morning.

He laughs and kisses her again.

ACT TWO

Scene One

The bath is still running. Music plays. Something simple and guitar-based.

MARIAN *is shaving her legs in a dressing gown with her legs in the bath.*

MARIAN. I am the Lord of Hellfire.

She bites her lip, thinking.

And I have come for your legs.

Her phone rings.

She looks at it.

She doesn't answer it.

She stands, half-shaved, and turns and looks at her (knickered) arse in the mirror, lifting her dressing gown to do so. She frowns. She stands on the edge of the bath to get a better look in the mirror. She frowns.

Mummy… what's a Lord of Hellfire?

She answers in a deep voice.

I – fucking – am.

She laughs. And then doesn't.

Scene Two

DAVID *is on the phone, he is now half-dressed, as he talks he stares at his hair. He brushes it forwards. No difference. He brushes it back. No difference.*

DAVID. We're a young company with an aggressive...

He opens the medicine cabinet.

No, no, that's fine...

He roots around at the back of it.

Well, we've had some concrete bites, if that makes sense, and actually we're going in today to...

He takes out some hair gel.

I could email you some thoughts... I can't keep... I'm late for my... I'm late so... yeah, I'd probably just...

And some contraceptive medication falls out with it.

He looks at it.

He looks again.

Great. Great. I'll do that.

He disconnects the call – he thinks.

He puts everything back in the cupboard.

Scene Three

MARIAN *stands on the scales and weighs herself.*

She looks at the scales. She stands off them.

She takes a breath. She holds her breath.

She stands on the scales.

She opens her mobile.

MARIAN. Hi, it's me...

    Yeah. I'm in the bathroom...

    Just standing on the bathroom scales...

    Weighing myself...

    To see how heavy I am...

    I know I'm thin...

    I know I'm thin...

    No. I don't...

    No. I won't...

    Mum.

    Yeah.

    Are you in the mood for a...?

    Yeah, so...

    David's at work...

    Yeah. I just want to go with someone...

    I don't know...

    Put down some flowers...

    Yeah. Now?

    I'll get the flowers...

    Okay.

She disconnects her mobile.

She stands looking at the scales.

Scene Four

DAVID *is sitting (fully clothed in a suit) on the toilet. It's now evening.*

He has his head in his hands. He's talking on a hands-free.

DAVID. We're just out of a pitch and, uh… We've had a number of bites and… well, angels and… well, more firm offers and we're looking for specific… We do have a PDF with some…

He takes off his tie.

Well, in the pitch just now actually the thing that excited them was our… Great. Great. What's your email…

He takes out a pen, he looks around for something to write on – he begins to write on the toilet roll.

Scene Five

DAVID *enters in a dressing gown and turns off the bath.*

He exits.

He enters again with tea lights.

He begins to light them. He places them throughout the room. What was a bathroom becomes a lair. Becomes a beautiful spot. Becomes somewhere with intensity to it.

A phone rings from off.

He listens to it.

DAVID. One alligator.

Two alligator.

Three alligator.

Four alligator.

It rings off.

He finishes lighting candles.

He looks around the room.

He exits.

He re-enters with some Febreze spray. He squirts it sort of artfully around the room. He smells the air. Then he smiles.

The fuck am I doing?

He thinks and then shuts the door.

He takes off his dressing gown. He's naked underneath.

He looks at himself in the mirror. He gives himself the appraising eye.

He turns around to look at his arse. He can't get a great angle in the mirror. He clenches his arse. He thinks. He clenches his arse again.

He turns back forward. He pushes his dick sideways. He does it again. He plays with his dick slightly so that it's bigger.

MARIAN *enters the room.*

I didn't hear you.

Beat.

MARIAN. I was quiet. I'm quite quiet.

What's this?

DAVID. It's for you. It's for us.

It's for you.

MARIAN. You're naked.

DAVID. I am.

Beat.

MARIAN. Why? Why are there candles here?

DAVID. For you.

MARIAN. You're naked – for me – and there are candles – also
for me?

Beat.

DAVID. You're early.

I wasn't expecting you yet. I thought I'd hear you. This isn't
exactly how I hoped this would go.

MARIAN. You really didn't hear me?

DAVID. No.

Pause.

MARIAN. Brought up by Indians.

DAVID. Yeah?

MARIAN. American Indians. I mean, quiet feet. Is that racist?

DAVID. Yeah.

Pause.

Hi.

MARIAN. Hi.

DAVID. You look nice. Your hair…

MARIAN. No.

DAVID. It looks different.

MARIAN. Are you leaving your dressing gown off?

DAVID. It looks different.

MARIAN. New shampoo.

I suspect.

Are you going to fuck me?

DAVID. No… Not…

MARIAN. Because as foreplay goes, nudity isn't especially subtle.

DAVID.…Unless you want to?

MARIAN. No.

And your penis is bigger than usual so that means you've been having some thoughts which are also not entirely subtle.

DAVID. No, I, uh, all I wanted to do is – I poured you a bath. I've got a… I've got… there is wine downstairs. Hold on.

MARIAN. Okay.

He exits.

She stands a moment.

Looking utterly lost.

She begins to cry.

He re-enters. She stops crying. He doesn't notice.

He picks up his gown and puts it on.

DAVID. Running through the house naked feels a little…

MARIAN. Flagrant.

DAVID. Exactly.

Entirely flagrant. Is that the right word?

MARIAN. Yes.

DAVID. White or red?

MARIAN. Red.

DAVID. Really?

MARIAN. Or white if you want white…

DAVID. Red's fine.

I'm just… red's fine.

DAVID exits again.

MARIAN stands a moment again.

She makes to decide whether she wants to cry or not.

She decides not.

Pause.

She makes a quick decision.

She takes off her clothes as rapidly as possible.

And then stands a moment, breathes, looks at herself in the mirror, and then climbs into the bath.

DAVID re-enters, clutching a wine bottle, and two slightly oversized wine glasses.

He's surprised to see her inside the bath.

You got in…

MARIAN. Yeah.

Beat.

DAVID. I was going to undress you.

Beat.

MARIAN. Were you?

Beat.

DAVID. I thought it might be nice…

Beat.

MARIAN. Like a mother and child.

Gently easing my clothes off of me.

Singing to me reassuring songs about farm equipment as you do.

DAVID *looks at her, not sure what she means, she looks back, not sure what she means either.*

DAVID. No, not that so much… more…

I don't know.

Farm equipment?

MARIAN. My mother had an odd idea of what was reassuring.

He looks at her.

DAVID. Wine?

MARIAN. Wein?

DAVID *smiles. He begins to open the bottle of wine.*

DAVID. Ja, wein?

MARIAN. Is it German?

DAVID. No. French.

She nods.

He pours her a glass.

In fact, madam… Now this, madam, is from our premiere range of French wines.

It cost a whole six pounds. Savour the tastes and smells. It smells like?

Yes. Tesco.

MARIAN. You're funny.

Beat. He's not.

DAVID. You're not laughing.

MARIAN. You're not that funny.

Beat.

DAVID. Room for a small one?

MARIAN. You're not that small.

DAVID. I'm smaller than you.

MARIAN. A lot of people are smaller than me. You didn't put enough bubbles in this bath.

DAVID. No.

MARIAN. I can't cover myself as much as I'd – like.

DAVID. You look great.

He takes his dressing gown off. He climbs into the bath.

It takes them a while to get comfortable.

If you put that there…

MARIAN. Like…

DAVID. Yeah.

MARIAN. Just move that…

DAVID. Yeah. Is that?

MARIAN. Yes, that's my vagina…

DAVID. So if I just…

MARIAN. Still my vagina…

DAVID. Hang on… I'll just…

MARIAN. Perfect.

They get comfortable. They're facing each other in the bath. He has his back to the taps.

He looks at her. She looks at him. She suddenly laughs.

DAVID. What?

MARIAN. Nothing.

DAVID. Okay.

But this bit deserves a laugh so…

She laughs again.

MARIAN. Sorry. It is quite…

DAVID. Why is that?

MARIAN. No, don't, it's lovely – jolly…

DAVID. Yeah.

MARIAN. Besides, I needed to laugh so…

DAVID. I was kind of looking forward to undressing you.

MARIAN. Were you?

DAVID. Yeah.

Pause. MARIAN *grins and starts singing the theme to* Record Breakers, *this is clearly a bit of a routine for them.*

She looks at DAVID, *she nods at him. He smiles – and then sings the next couple of lines with slight reluctance. They sing the last few lines together.*

They finish and both smile.

MARIAN. How was the presentation?

DAVID. They want us to come back with more figures. How was here?

MARIAN. More or less the same. The cat vomited.

So that was exciting.

I'm thinking of starting work again…

DAVID. Yeah?

Pause.

MARIAN. Only if you think…

Pause.

DAVID. Yeah.

Pause.

It's strange what you want permission for and what you don't.

MARIAN. Is it?

DAVID. Yeah.

MARIAN. What does that mean?

DAVID. I mean… I mostly mean, people generally, not – you…

MARIAN. Okay.

DAVID. This didn't start as I hoped.

MARIAN. No.

DAVID. I didn't expect you to find it funny.

Pause. MARIAN *thinks.*

MARIAN. What does 'more figures' mean?

DAVID. It means they need more information…

MARIAN. Everyone always needs more information.

DAVID. Yes. But they want more before they…

MARIAN. Fire the gun.

DAVID. And we couldn't exactly – we couldn't exactly demand an answer.

They know we're…

MARIAN. Weak.

DAVID. Exactly.

MARIAN. Not in a bad way.

DAVID. No. No. We've just got small… horses.

Pause.

MARIAN. You remember that time I got the squits in Zimbabwe?

DAVID. Not now I don't.

Now I'm choosing to forget such a moment.

MARIAN. No?

Okay. Just trying to be nostalgic… in the bath…

DAVID. We don't have the memories for nostalgia.

MARIAN. I know.

DAVID. Neither of us do. It's – we've never remembered anything…

MARIAN. And my nostalgia literally mostly relates to pooing and shitting. Which isn't really a nostalgia we can enjoy together considering your aversion to my pooing and shitting. I use both words. Why use one when two can do? Pooing and shitting. Now, that would be a great name for a band.

Pause.

First time you had your heart broken…

DAVID. What's wrong with just being a bit quiet?

MARIAN. Close your eyes. First time you felt like you were going to succeed at something, first time you can remember true fear, first time you felt intentional love for someone or something, first time you picked up an animal and realised you could kill it, first time you used the toilet in front of someone who wasn't helping you, first time you realised eating chocolate was bad, first time you had sexual feelings for a teacher, first time you had sexual feelings for someone you knew you shouldn't have sexual feelings for, first time you farted in a lift, first time you intentionally farted in a lift, first time you masturbated, first time you realised you weren't always going to have friends, first time you realised your friends weren't good enough, first time you felt genuine despair, first time you rode a bike without hands, first time you felt true shame, first time you pissed in a bath and meant it, first time you realised you were cleverer than other people, first time you realised you weren't as clever as you realised, first time you felt like your life had changed unutterably, first time you clearly remember lying, first time you remember giving someone something you didn't want to give, first time you had your heart broken…

You didn't close your eyes.

DAVID. No.

MARIAN. Pity.

DAVID. Yes.

MARIAN. Secondary school.

He was called Peter.

DAVID. Peter. I hate him already.

MARIAN. Because he was called Peter?

DAVID. Parents who name their kids Peter – it's generally, maybe subconsciously or… but it's generally after St Peter.

I think that's arrogant. Tell me more.

MARIAN. He was in a band.

DAVID. Drummer?

MARIAN. Drummer! Do I look like the sort of girl who'd date the drummer?

Guitarist.

Bass guitarist.

DAVID. Sexy.

MARIAN. Deadly sexy.

Brown eyes. Sculpted arms.

He had – what do you call that haircut that boys – he had curtains.

DAVID. Now I do hate him

MARIAN. Hair fascist.

DAVID. Yeah.

MARIAN. Wasn't Peter a shit saint? Denying Christ and…

DAVID. Only at that bit. And he needed to be. The rest of the time he was brilliant.

MARIAN. He called me 'his crumpet' – I think that was his attempt to be Cockney Gangster.

DAVID. Cockney Gangster?

MARIAN. I know, what did we know, we were at posh school, you were actually a – your granddad met Reggie Kray.

DAVID. Ronnie Kray.

MARIAN. Same difference.

DAVID. And he didn't 'meet' Ronnie, he stood up to Ronnie.

You were – you always get that story slightly wrong...

MARIAN. Were we talking about me?

DAVID. We were. You and the bass guitarist.

MARIAN *splashes* DAVID *with some water.*

MARIAN. Pour me some more wine.

Beat.

DAVID. Of course.

DAVID *does.*

MARIAN. This was nice of you.

To do the bath thing.

Sorry I laughed.

DAVID. Yeah?

Beat.

MARIAN. So the meeting was a write-off, a total write-off...

DAVID. Not a total write-off.

We've got another meeting.

MARIAN. Which will be your...

DAVID. Fourth.

They want projected international sales. They want breakdowns on parts.

They want to know assimilation costs and...

MARIAN. What did Paul...?

DAVID. 'We should have ended with the figures, if we'd ended with our figures they wouldn't have wanted more – figures.'

I don't want to talk about it.

You were telling me about Pete…

MARIAN. I was…

DAVID. Pistol Pete the bass guitarist.

MARIAN. I was.

DAVID. A man I love to hate.

MARIAN. He's now friends with me on Facebook.

DAVID. Is he married?

MARIAN. No.

DAVID. Is he fat?

MARIAN. No. Less hair though.

DAVID. Right.

MARIAN. Don't smile.

Pete and I first started going out on the biology field trip to Dartmoor.

DAVID. Dartmoor?

MARIAN. Was it biology?

May have been geography… Very interesting stones.

Stones.

I remember us having to look at stones. I don't know.

There wasn't even a gift shop so we were forced to spend all our money at a service station. He kissed me beside the fizzy-drinks fridge.

DAVID. Sounds romantic.

MARIAN. Very romantic.

I touched his hair.

He put his tongue in my mouth.

DAVID. Nice.

MARIAN. It was a tumultuous relationship.

Riven through with deceit, intrigue and band practice.

DAVID. I think I may be getting an erection.

Beat. She smiles.

MARIAN. We split up at Thomas Jenkins's house party.

DAVID. Thomas Jenkins's house party? Once again your school years sound like the Famous Five.

MARIAN. Thomas Jenkins was a cunt.

DAVID. Ah.

MARIAN. Did they have house parties in the Famous Five?

DAVID. No. But…

MARIAN. I thought they just ate ham sandwiches, drank ginger beer and didn't notice that girl having a gender crisis…

DAVID. George.

MARIAN. Now how did you remember that name – do you fancy her? You fancy fat girls and girls having a gender crisis.

DAVID. I never fancied George.

MARIAN. Thomas Jenkins tried to stick four fingers up my friend Shona.

She was in quite a lot of pain. She screamed. He didn't like her screaming.

Called her frigid and tight. There was some sort of play on words, her name and the word tight… Or…

DAVID. We hate Thomas Jenkins…

MARIAN. Slippery Shona.

Everyone called her Slippery Shona. To be fair, I may have called her Slippery Shona. The cricket team called her First Slip.

DAVID. Cricket team? Famous fucking Five.

MARIAN. You didn't have a cricket team?

DAVID. No.

MARIAN. Man of the people. Fucker of fat girls. I doff my hat.

DAVID. Thanks.

MARIAN. This wine is fine.

DAVID. Better than I thought it would be.

Beat.

MARIAN. Anyway – that night – Lizzie, year above, bit fat, terrible slut – you'd have loved her – gave Pistol Pete a blowie in Thomas Jenkins's garage beside Thomas Jenkins's dad's vintage Mazda.

DAVID. Can you – is there such a thing as a vintage Mazda?

MARIAN. Is that the point of my story?

DAVID. And you found them?

MARIAN. No… No… Not that kind of story…

No. He just told everyone.

Getting a blowjob was quite an achievement in those days…

DAVID. I can imagine.

Beat.

MARIAN. First heartbreak. I was fourteen.

I shagged Steve Bryson ten months later. Mainly to show I wasn't frigid like Shona and that I hated Pete.

DAVID. Fourteen?

MARIAN. I may have been fifteen by then.

We had sex in the public-school system too you know…

Pause.

You don't want to talk about it? At all?

DAVID. Pistol Pete?

MARIAN. The meeting.

DAVID. There's nothing to talk about…

MARIAN. But…

DAVID. I've basically told you everything.

MARIAN. I am in control of all the information.

DAVID. You are.

MARIAN. Go on then. First heartbreak.

DAVID. I'm not very good at this game…

MARIAN. All the same…

DAVID. Really? Can't we…

MARIAN. We can talk about your meeting or your first heartbreak. One or the other…

DAVID. I was considerably older.

MARIAN. That's okay.

DAVID. I was twenty. University.

MARIAN. This is all okay.

DAVID. Her name was Rachel Annes.

MARIAN. No, I already know about her.

DAVID. Well. She was…

MARIAN. The game is no fun if I already know about someone…

Beat.

DAVID. Well. That's what she was… She was my first heartbreak.

MARIAN. Yeah, well, there you go.

You were supposed to tell me something new.

That wasn't something new.

DAVID. You know me pretty well… No new information.

MARIAN. Did you know about Pete?

DAVID. Pistol Pete, the blowjob king?

No.

But you've had lots of boyfriends.

MARIAN. Well, yes, I have.

DAVID. Your information source is – wider – than mine.

I've had less girlfriends.

MARIAN. Yes. You have.

That's because you're sullen.

DAVID. 'Sullen'?

MARIAN. Girls don't go for sullen men.

DAVID. I wish I'd known that sooner…

Why are our conversations so inconsequential?

MARIAN. One thing I like about you is your ability to grenade-bomb me with words more than two syllables. You don't do it often. But I always appreciate it.

Pause.

DAVID. I thought I was quite full of life…

MARIAN. You're dynamic.

DAVID. I'll take dynamic.

MARIAN. And sullen.

Rachel Annes.

Two first names instead of one.

The girl was always cursed to fall in love with a sullen man like you.

Pause.

DAVID. Yeah?

Beat.

MARIAN. Yeah.

Have you told me about all the fat girls?

Which ones were fat?

DAVID. Yeah yeah. Shit game really.

MARIAN. Only when I play it with you.

DAVID. I've told you about all of them. Fat and thin.

MARIAN. Okay.

DAVID. Shit game, you see…

MARIAN. Okay. So…

Okay.

Pause.

DAVID. Are you taking the pill?

Beat.

MARIAN. What?

DAVID. Are you taking birth control?

Talking of information.

Shall we talk about that…

MARIAN. Talk about what?

DAVID. Because I thought we agreed…

MARIAN. Thought we agreed what?

DAVID. That we were trying again…

MARIAN. When did we agree that…?

DAVID. We agreed that…

MARIAN. You agreed that.

DAVID. We did.

MARIAN. No. I still I was still – she was my – I didn't want a replacement just yet.

Pause.

Was that what this bath was about?

DAVID. Don't turn this…

MARIAN. Because I thought this bath was about you reaching
out to me, we'd have an emotional bath, discuss things of
inconsequence and go to bed and I'd sit on your face. But
instead –

DAVID. I didn't want a replacement.

MARIAN. But instead this is an interrogation room, isn't it?

DAVID. I didn't want a replacement.

Beat. She looks up at his face.

MARIAN. Yes.

I'm taking…

Actually I am.

I'm taking. Yeah.

Beat.

DAVID. And you kept it from me?

MARIAN *looks at him.*

MARIAN. I didn't advertise it.

DAVID. You didn't mention it.

MARIAN. I just let you cum inside me under false pretences.
Yes.

Sue my womb for flagrant lying. I apologise to all your
unnecessary spermatozoa.

It's my body.

I didn't want to have an argument.

DAVID. So you let me hope?

MARIAN. I weigh the same. My arse isn't bigger.

DAVID. You let me hope?

I mean, of information that can be…

MARIAN. Looking at me all the time trying to work out when
I'm going to deliver you version fucking two. Your much
needed sequel.

DAVID. You let me hope. That was… that is… information I'd have…

MARIAN. My arse is exactly the same.

And don't even start to – don't even start to – when was the last time you went to her grave?

I had to go with my fucking mother.

DAVID. You let me hope.

MARIAN. No, I let you fuck me.

You did all the hoping by yourself.

Pause.

DAVID *makes to say something.*

And then says nothing.

DAVID. Okay. Here's something that you…

Pause.

Okay. Here's information…

Pause.

When I was at school – I got picked for my – can't have been more than twelve – got picked for my school's football team. Right-back.

It was a big moment for me.

Even bigger one for my dad. Because – um – because he was my dad and that's what they… He always said the reason why he didn't play football professionally was racism, he went for a few trials – he was shit.

The reason why he didn't play football professionally was – he was shit. But anyway, me being picked for my school football team. That mattered.

I was pretty shit too.

But I was willing and would run around a lot. And that's pretty much all you need to be a right-back.

MARIAN. I don't know much about football.

Beat.

DAVID. I know you don't. Anyway, I arranged to meet my friend Tony before the game. We said we were going to warm up together. He was making his debut too.

We went to the chip shop and bought a packet of chips which we shared. I remember it quite clearly. He put too much salt on the chips.

They tasted like shit.

Tony was a midfielder. Quite good. Sort of a midfield marauder but with a bit of elegance. Sort of Paul Ince-like.

MARIAN. I don't know much about football.

DAVID. Anyway, after about five minutes, these girls came over and started talking and, uh… We talked back. And then they left.

And then a couple of older lads with their own car – came over and gave us a couple of cigarettes…

MARIAN. You smoked?

DAVID. And then…

MARIAN. You always hate me smoking.

DAVID. And they said, we've heard about this thing – there's this old car up the rec and some kids are going to set fire to it you want to come watch?

We were due at school in about five minutes but Tony said 'yeah'. Immediately he said 'yeah'. And I said nothing. We drove up there. There wasn't anything on fire. The older boys said 'fuck it, that's annoying' and we said 'yeah'.

They didn't offer us a lift back. So we missed the football.

My dad asked afterwards whether I'd been ill. He was working nights at the time – couldn't get a better job – he took the night off to watch me play. I never made the team again.

Tony did.

Actually, Tony was eventually made captain.

You want to know when I first had my heart broke? Then. I was… I broke my own heart. That's what – that's what. I broke my own heart.

DAVID *sits for ages.*

DAVID *leans across. He touches* MARIAN's *face.*

And then he thinks. And then he starts to push her down.

He starts to push her down. Under the water.

MARIAN. No… No… David… David…

He pushes her down under the water.

He holds her for what seems like too long.

He holds for what seems like way too long.

He holds her to the point where most would assume she's dead.

And then he stops.

And she re-emerges.

Breathing deeply.

And she makes to hurt him but realises he's not going to hurt her. And so doesn't.

And he looks at her. And she looks back.

And this lasts for fucking ever.

Right then.

They look at each other with deadly accuracy.

And then he stands up.

And he walks out of the bath and away.

Out of the room.

Dripping water as he goes.

Scene Six

MARIAN *gets out of the bath – she sits on the edge of the bath – lit only by candles. She sings something gently to herself. We don't hear what it is.*

Then she stands, picks up a towel and wraps it carefully around herself.

She leaves the bathroom.

Scene Seven

DAVID *enters, he looks around the room, he unplugs the bath, which begins to drain out.*

He looks at himself in the mirror.

He blows all the candles out.

He picks them up. He takes them out with him. A phone begins to ring in the background.

ACT THREE

Scene One

Lights rise on an empty bathroom.

The taps dripping.

DAVID (*from off*). Marian… Marian…

> *Lights fall.*

Scene Two

Lights rise.

DAVID (*from off*). Marian… Marian…

> DAVID *enters the bathroom.*

> Marian… Marian…

> *Beat. He looks around.*

> *His phone rings. He looks at it.*

> *Beat. He answers it.*

> Hi. Did you get the brochure?… Yeah, we're really excited –
> we're trying to… You're not?… No… Well, I think if you…
> No. If it's not right for you… Thanks for letting me know.

> *Beat. He disconnects the call. He sits on the floor.*

> *Beat.*

> *He looks at his phone.*

> *He makes a call.*

> *He waits.*

His face drops.

You know I hate answerphones. Where are you?

He disconnects.

He looks around the room. He stands – not sure what to do.

Beat. Lights down.

Scene Three

MARIAN *sits on the floor by the toilet and speaks in the softest voice.*

MARIAN. Because I'm okay, Mum…

I'm actually okay so…

No, I don't want you to come over…

No, I don't want you to come over…

Because I'm okay…

Yes, I am…

Mum, please, I didn't call you so you'd be all fucking pugilistic about it…

Pugilistic…

It's a word…

I like being 'flowery'…

Then just…

Is that the important thing right now…?

Mum…

It's just today…

It's late…

Yeah.

MARIAN *disconnects.*

She sits for an age.

Then she puts on her headphones.

Vous l'avez en magasin?

Vous l'avez en magasin?

Beat. She stands, she stretches, she creaks, she takes some face cream out of the cupboard and begins to apply it.

Quel est votre dernier prix?

Quel est votre dernier prix?

Beat.

Vous me faites un prix d'ami?

Vous me faites un prix d'ami?

DAVID *enters the bathroom. He's carrying a glass with whisky in it.*

MARIAN *turns off the iPod and takes off the headphones.*

They stand there for a moment.

Pause.

DAVID. I've called Paul.

Beat.

MARIAN. Right.

DAVID. I've told him I'm not coming in tomorrow…

Beat.

MARIAN. Right.

Pause.

DAVID. I thought we could take a trip.

And I'm sort of…

The main problem is we're trying to sell something no one wants. We're pretty good at selling it. But that's our main problem.

Pause.

I mean, it's mainly you, my – main – sole really reason for taking the day is – you.

I thought we could take a trip.

MARIAN. Right. Where?

Pause.

DAVID. To – a forest or a beach or something…

MARIAN. Right. Okay.

DAVID. Or a – we could go walking or just – eat somewhere and… Or just do something. We could even go to a cinema. I don't know the last time was when I saw a film during the day. I imagine it'll feel quite – odd.

Do you want that? A trip, I mean, not – the cinema – necessarily…

MARIAN. Yeah. Maybe.

DAVID. I'm sorry.

Beat. His face breaks as if it's about to cry and then he controls himself.

I feel like I've cut my arm off or something.

I feel like I should cut my arm off or something.

I'm really sorry.

MARIAN. I know.

Beat.

DAVID. Sometimes I sit in a room and I just feel…

Today I sat in a room – surrounded by people and it just looked like they were all – talking.

You know how sometimes it can look like everyone is talking all at once.

How everyone is talking all the time. And you're just – trying to –

Sometimes I sit in a room and I feel like I'm not in a room.

It's funny isn't it – missing something – missing something when you're not sure what the thing would now – be.

I don't know.

It's not about me.

I love you.

MARIAN. Okay.

DAVID. I do.

MARIAN. I know.

DAVID. You're so beautiful.

You make me feel lucky. But, uh…

You're so beautiful.

Beat.

MARIAN. Thanks.

DAVID. But it's always been too important to me that you're beautiful.

Sometimes I look at you and you don't look the way I hoped. Sometimes I look at you and you do.

MARIAN. I think that's normal.

DAVID. But it shouldn't matter so much.

MARIAN. No. That's true.

DAVID. I don't really know what I'm saying…

Do you love me?

MARIAN. Yes.

DAVID. You do?

MARIAN. If you ask a question, David, and I answer it, there's
no need to reassure yourself of the – answer.

Pause.

DAVID. Where did you… Where have you been?

Beat.

MARIAN. I went for a walk.

Beat.

DAVID. Yeah?

Beat.

MARIAN. Yes. I heard some kids were setting fire to a car up
the rec. So I thought I'd…

DAVID. I heard you talking.

MARIAN. My French tape.

DAVID. I've never totally understood your French tape…

I mean, I support you, in it, extending the brain and… but…

MARIAN. Because it's where I want – old people have a good
time over there – it's where I want to die.

DAVID. You want to die in France?

MARIAN. Have I not said before…?

DAVID. No.

MARIAN. But we're not good at remembering, so I could have
and…

DAVID. True.

MARIAN. Just to clarify, when you say you're sorry –

DAVID. Very.

MARIAN. Just to clarify – for which bit – are you sorry?

Pause. DAVID *considers.*

You can go in – to work tomorrow. You should go in to work
tomorrow. Work will require you tomorrow.

You have figures. You have information to…

DAVID. All of it. I'm sorry for all of it.

MARIAN. That's a shit answer. Specifically – for which bit of today –

DAVID. I don't know which bit.

MARIAN. Okay. You don't? That's – strange.

DAVID. No, I just – for all of it…

MARIAN. Did you want to kill me? Are you sorry for that? Sorry that you didn't?

DAVID. No. I didn't want to kill you.

MARIAN. Then what did you want?

DAVID. I wanted you to stop.

I think.

I don't know.

MARIAN. I wasn't talking.

DAVID. I wanted you to stop being there.

Yeah. I wanted you to stop.

You used to say it was something good about us – that there were things we forgot. Like what we did last week. We only knew – you used to say – we only knew that there were… that good things happened last night. You said you'd forget our anniversary if you didn't have an alert on your phone.

MARIAN. I know.

But things have become easier to remember.

Pause.

Sometimes. I used to have a dream –

DAVID. Not another dream…

MARIAN. All the time that was about you cutting open – cutting me open, taking a pair of scissors and putting one half inside my vagina –

DAVID. I hate your dreams…

MARIAN. And cutting me open – from there on up. Big scissors. Dress-making scissors.

I have that dream all the time.

More than the masturbating grass people. I have that one all the time. Never told you about that.

Never told you about that or my desire to die in France.

Where old people are – old people have a good time in France.

Boules and cards and coffee and weather and…

Pause. DAVID *opens his mouth to speak. And then closes it again. A tear drips from one of their faces.*

When she… When you… When she… You just had a fucking – look – on your – when she – you had this look on your – face. And that look… that fucking look…

DAVID. I can't stop how my face works.

MARIAN. Of course you can. You don't think I don't…? You don't think my face doesn't…

DAVID. I can't.

I'm not as clever as you. I can't.

MARIAN. You looked like you wanted to spit at me. For being so fucking – defective.

DAVID. Did I?

MARIAN. Football team? You missed a game? You missed a game for your football team?

DAVID. It was – I was being metaphorical.

MARIAN. Were you?

DAVID. No. Yes. I don't know. I was being historical. I don't know. I'm not as clever as you. Well educated. I don't know.

Pause. MARIAN *sits on the bath.* DAVID *thinks, and then sits beside her.*

I didn't go to the grave today...

MARIAN. No...

DAVID. I didn't go to the grave today.

MARIAN. No. Don't finish that thought. No excuses.

DAVID. You never listen to me.

MARIAN. Yes. I do actually. I do listen. All the time.

Pause.

You wanted me to stop?

Sometimes I want me to stop too.

And sometimes I want you to stop.

DAVID. I know.

Pause.

MARIAN. The worst thing is... I think – I liked – you – hurting me.

DAVID *looks up and says nothing*. MARIAN *says nothing. The words settle.*

I'm not sure though.

DAVID. Yeah?

Pause.

MARIAN. And that. And that. Don't know what that all means. Catch me next week, folks, to – find – out.

Pause. She can't look at him. He can't look at her.

And you may think my dreams are bad or boring – but you – you grind your teeth and shake in the night so whatever you're... Whatever's going on in that head of yours... Probably it's just about football games.

I'm sorry you missed your football game.

Pause. She turns slowly to look at him. He tries to look back.

Anyway. Anyway. So we need a… So do we… Should we? Can we try it again some time? You hurting me? Can we try that again?

DAVID. What?

MARIAN. I think we should try that thing again.

You hurting me again.

DAVID. What? N…

MARIAN. It's better for you and like I say, I think I like it too.

DAVID. No. I don't…

MARIAN. That way we can both – stop.

DAVID. No…

MARIAN. And actually it made today easier because it stopped the clock in my brain and – for a moment I hated you more than I missed her.

DAVID. I miss – her – too.

MARIAN. So can we try it again? Some time.

Can we try you hurting me again some time? Can we try that? You liked it too, right?

DAVID *looks at her.*

Pause. She doesn't look back.

DAVID. Marian…

Pause. She still doesn't look back.

Marian…

Pause. She still doesn't look back.

Marian…

She looks up at him. They look at each other for too long. He stands and moves away from her. He touches the floor. He doesn't know why. He frowns.

We're going to be okay, you and me, we're going to be okay.

MARIAN. Why?

Pause.

DAVID. Because I can make things right again.

MARIAN. You…

DAVID. I want to be. I think we should be. I just want to be hopeful.

MARIAN. No. You want to be forgetful.

DAVID. No.

MARIAN. Sometimes – don't you think – there was a chance – and we missed it?

DAVID. Yeah. So we now – now we need to make a new chance…

MARIAN. Not make…

DAVID. No. No. I don't mean… I just mean we need to… Try harder to be… Try harder.

MARIAN. Why?

DAVID. Because what else are we going to do.

Pause. MARIAN *considers.*

I'm sorry I tried to… I'm sorry I hurt you. I'm really sorry. And I won't do it again. And I'm – I don't know. And if I do – if I do – I'll kill myself.

MARIAN. Sales pitch.

DAVID. Truth.

Pause. MARIAN *considers.*

MARIAN. Okay.

DAVID. We're going to take a day trip tomorrow. Fuck Paul. Fuck work. Go back to somewhere we remember. Some nice – place.

MARIAN. Okay.

DAVID. Go to that pub in Richmond that does the roasts on the big plates... Go to the park, look at the deer, go to the pub...

MARIAN. Okay. It's not Sunday tomorrow...

DAVID. No. Good point.

MARIAN. So a roast would be...

DAVID. Yeah.

MARIAN. I mean, they probably only get the plates out on...

DAVID. Sunday. Yeah.

Pause. MARIAN *looks up.*

MARIAN. And I'd rather go somewhere new.

DAVID. Okay.

MARIAN. I'd rather go to somewhere new.

Pause.

DAVID. Yes. New is better.

Pause.

Maybe we should go to the cinema...

Maybe we should go to France...

Pause. MARIAN *smiles.*

MARIAN. Maybe we should.

DAVID. And play cards and bowls.

MARIAN. Boules.

DAVID. Bowls.

Pause.

She smiles.

MARIAN. Bowls.

Pause. He sits beside her on the edge of the bath.

DAVID. And if that doesn't work we'll just… hope that…

MARIAN. Yeah.

MARIAN smiles, DAVID smiles, and then they don't.

DAVID. Are you hungry?

I haven't eaten.

Are you hungry?

Talk of the roast has made me… I could fix us some – I can fix us something…

Eggs or noodles or…

We've got those Linda McCartney frozen lasagnes in that your mum said…

They're not too bad.

Pause.

She looks carefully at his face.

MARIAN. Yeah. I think…

Maybe…

We deserve each other.

DAVID. Do we?

MARIAN. Information gatherers. Information deleterers. Information… what's the opposite of information? Misinformation?

DAVID. Ignorance?

Pause. MARIAN considers this. She looks at her hands and then up at him.

MARIAN. You'll hurt me again. Just so you know. You will.

And I'll probably be quite forgiving. Again.

Because we deserve each other.

Beat. DAVID looks at her. And says nothing.

Yeah, I can be fed – I'm hungry…

And actually – I'd quite like to get drunk.

The End.